People, Parks & Cities

A guide to current good practice in urban parks

March 1996

A Report for the
Department of the Environment

By Liz Greenhalgh & Ken Worpole (Comedia)
in association with Robin Grove-White
(Centre for the Study of Environmental Change, Lancaster University)
& Tom Lonsdale (Camlin Lonsdale)

London: HMSO

ISBN 0 11 753258 4

Contents

1. Introduction

2. Summary of Good Practice

3. Main Case - Studies

Supplementary case-studies

Acknowledgements

We are especially grateful to the following people for their help in this study: Marion Headicar, David Martin and Marie Pender of the Department of the Environment; Peter Boarder, Chris Burton, Lia Ghilardi, Naseem Khan, Francois Matarasso, John Newton and Sue Swingler for local research; Larraine Worpole for photography; Alan Barber of ILAM and Helen Goody of the AMA for support and encouragement; and finally the many individuals who gave time to speak to us and talk about the work they are currently doing in urban parks and other environmental spaces.

Executive Summary

There is a strong tradition of municipal park provision in the UK contributing, historically, to the health and enjoyment of urban populations. In recent times, the circumstances of provision have changed, both among providers and users, and there is a need to think more imaginatively about what kinds of urban parks and environmental spaces modern towns and cities need.

This report and guidance on good practice, is based on twelve main case-studies, supported by a further 26 supplementary case-studies. These case-studies highlight good practice in the following areas:

Planning: the need for information-based strategies for parks, detailing what spaces there are, their present function, patterns of use and future potential;

Managing: the use of multi-disciplinary teams to put together parks strategies that cover all aspects of modern park provision, including the need to integrate both indoor and outdoor leisure facilities;

Competing: how best to use the competitive tendering process to add value to parks and open spaces, and ensure good management as well as effective maintenance;

Delegating: exploring new forms of partnerships with community groups, as well as new organisational forms such as trusts, where appropriate;

Maintaining: creating robust spaces and places which are adaptable to changing needs;

Building: understanding that parks are not simply residual natural landscapes but were developed to meet social and recreational needs, some of which are enhanced by facilities, events and buildings;

Monitoring: understanding the 'how, why, when and where' of park use, and giving as much attention to monitoring use as is currently given to monitoring standards of maintenance;

Involving: looking at community development skills in parks provision, and encouraging local individuals and organisations to take an active part in the care and well-being of their local parks and open spaces;

Funding: exploring new sources of funding for open space provision, tapping into urban regeneration programmes, developing partnerships with other agencies in both the public and private sectors;

Moving on: promoting the value of urban parks and open spaces for contemporary needs such as health and environmental education and the growing understanding of the calls for greater urban sustainability.

Common themes

In addition to these specific areas of parks provision, there are three key aspects common to all of them which should guide the further development of urban green and open space in coming decades. These are:

Strategic thinking

The need for providing organisations to stay in touch with changing demographic, social, environmental and cultural trends, and to be flexible and responsive to new demands.

Partnerships

There is no doubt that in future parks will need to rely on a wider mix of resources, whether directly financial through other funding programmes, private sector sponsorship; or, perhaps most importantly, through the active, voluntary participation of local community and environmental organisations whose interest and sense of ownership will ultimately determine the success or failure of contemporary open spaces.

Parks as focal points

There is an invaluable role to be played by urban parks in forthcoming programmes dedicated to greater urban sustainability, as places where, almost uniquely, ecological, social, cultural and economic imperatives come together. Urban parks could be focal points for Agenda 21 policies.

It is hoped that this overview of current good practice will lead to a much wider exchange of views and sharing of better ways of working. For the town or city park remains a uniquely valued part of our urban landscape, and its contribution to the quality of life in our towns and cities - as the Victorians understood - is potentially inestimable.

Chapter 1. Introduction

Background

This report and guidance on good practice in the provision, management and maintenance of urban parks was commissioned by the Department of the Environment (DoE) in July 1995. It was a follow-up and response to the widespread interest occasioned by the publication in May 1995 of the Comedia/Demos report 'Park Life: Urban Parks and Social Renewal', which itself was used as the basis for a Department of Environment brochure 'Better Parks, Better Cities' published in June 1995.

Given the renewed interest in urban parks by bodies as diverse as the Institute of Leisure & Amenity Management (ILAM), the Landscape Institute, English Heritage, the Garden History Society, and the main local authority bodies such as the Association of Metropolitan Authorities (AMA) and the Association of District Councils (ADC), as well as within the DoE itself, there was a sense of urgency about pulling together examples of good practice for dissemination and debate. In addition the prospect of lottery funding dedicated to urban parks renewal, added to the concern to provide further evidence of good practice.

Local authority management

For more than a century, local government has been the custodian of the public park. However, in recent years, local authorities have been forced by statute and economic circumstances to review their arrangements for service provision including parks. The range of different types of parks for which local authorities are now responsible has expanded. The traditional town park is now complemented by recreation grounds, natural parks, walks and other types of open space. In the past, park management was seen to be synonymous with horticultural maintenance. The advances in park management over the last few years have been built on the recognition that there is more to the parks service than maintenance alone, and patterns of decline are now being reversed by good management and new funding arrangements.

Park management has also been affected by changes in the structure of cities and in patterns of urban living. Park managers have had to take account of changes in urban life; different leisure patterns; questions of fear and security in public places; provision for children; the use of parks as venues for open air events; concerns to protect wildlife and reduce pollution. Park managers have had to find ways to resolve conflict about how areas of public space should be used, whilst at the same time protecting the spirit of public parks as places of freedom. The past glory of the town park as an emblem of local power has given way to a more diverse (and more interesting) set of demands.

Is Agenda 21 the key?

Agenda 21 is the name of the programme of action for achieving more sustainable forms of development agreed at the 1992 'earth summit' in Rio de Janeiro. The programme assumes widespread consultation by local and national governments, and over 50% of local authorities in the UK are now drawing up their own action plans for local Agenda 21. It is being seen by a growing number of commentators as a potential umbrella under which newer forms of public engagement with environmental issues can be explored. Agenda 21 and the concept of urban sustainability present a substantial challenge to local government, helping it to explore new ways of working with outside partners including the voluntary sector, community groups and individuals. On the other hand, if Agenda 21 merely becomes a new official jargon for use primarily within government circles, then far from creating new opportunities it may well alienate individuals and community groups. Studies such as one commissioned by Lancashire County Council from the Centre for the Study of Environmental Change (CSEC) on 'Public Perceptions of Sustainability' throws light on the gap between official and popular understandings of terms such as 'sustainable development'.

How then might these various observations bear on the concerns of the present study ? As the Park Life study made clear, public parks in towns and cities have immense symbolic significance as residual shared goods 'owned' (in principle) by increasingly diversified urban populations. Hence parks, and debates about them, have the potential to become important focal points for new forms of shared engagement, consistent with the purposes of Agenda 21. They also offer a rare range of opportunities for local authorities themselves to learn how to forge new patterns of active relationships with local populations who feel increasingly - and disturbingly - disconnected from them, in the circumstances of modern Britain.

Agenda 21 may provide a framework to develop more adventurous approaches to those parks experiencing decline. It highlights an opportunity to create local coalitions between community groups, wildlife groups, residents groups, sports groups, environmentalists, dog owners, horticulturists and many others to discuss new uses and forms of management of local parks. The Lancashire County Council study found that for most people environmental and 'sustainability' issues were best understood and engaged with at intimate local levels. Arguably, public parks now have the potential to become an especially appropriate focus of public attention in just such terms. The examples of community involvement in this report highlight opportunities for creating consensus amongst different community groups about how to develop parks.

The key to success in any such endeavours will lie in the imagination and enterprise with which local authorities and others can frame

and stimulate new debates and ideas about the future of parks. Several pointers suggest themselves:

(a) Political priority

The strategic significance of parks issues both for overall community welfare and for Agenda 21 priorities means that debates about them should be given higher political priority, ideally with responsibility vested in the political leadership and Chief Executive's office of particular authorities.

(b) Planning the debates

Before initiating debates on particular parks, local authorities should explore, sensitively and in detail, the potential range of public interests and sensibilities.

(c) Harness new thinking

There is a growing debate on possible ways forward for local democracy in the UK. Some of this suggests new mechanisms for local authority interaction with citizens - for example, citizens' juries, consensus conferences, interactive town meetings, and festivals. The parks issue has the potential for the creative introduction of, and experimentation with, such approaches.

(d) Open-mindedness

The essence of these new approaches to negotiating the future of public parks should be a welcome acceptance of the unknowns implicit in the processes. It may well be that new forms of specialist or selective management in particular areas might be deemed appropriate. For example, it might emerge that particular parks were best 'handed over' to a limited range of specialist concerns - say, exclusively sport or nature conservation preoccupations - as a result of soundings taken under (b) above. Alternatively, a far wider range of interests than hitherto thought relevant might emerge. The important point is that the opportunity exists for fresh and creative thought. It is hoped that this report will help stimulate this kind of creative thinking.

What is meant by good practice?

The possibilities for imaginative uses of urban parks are inexhaustible. They can be:

◆ Adapted for educational uses;

◆ Tied into health policies;

◆ Used to expand opportunities for leisure, sport and to provide varied play for children;

◆ Places that allow for voluntary involvement in conservation and many other projects;

◆ Sites for community facilities;

◆ A focus to strengthen local connections, networks and experiments in projects to enhance local democratic control;

◆ Used as places for training, even possibly creating some employment opportunities and commercial enterprises.

It is even feasible that parks could have a role in managing urban waste and rainwater and providing safe (non-road based) networks for connecting up the city.

In reality, urban parks are limited by existing constraints: whether these are financial (particularly for revenue spending and competition for grant allocations); or urban problems associated with crime and the fear of crime, or whether they take the form of legal or managerial pressures. No single local authority can demonstrate good practice in every area. 'Good practice' or guidelines for urban parks might suggest a set of rules that if followed will lead to such an ideal. Such an ideal does not exist, nor should it. There is no single model or 'the right path' to follow. Indeed, the real opportunity for urban parks is to open up to new possibilities and new demands, not to close them down by following pre-determined paths.

Every park is different. Each local situation is specific. Every town or city embodies a unique mix of history, political networks, topography and organisational capacity. Therefore we have avoided providing a prescriptive, schematic approach to good practice, which would suggest the easy transferability of any single model of development from one place to another. There is no formula for instant success,

whether in developing strategies, securing greater community involvement or raising additional funds. Every local authority or any other kind of parks agency will have to find its own solution. This report sets out to expand the range of ideas of what is possible, what can be achieved, and how different kinds of common problems can be solved. Its aim is to raise people's sights beyond the day to day problems, to help them learn from each other, and also to be a source of inspiration.

While we cannot be prescriptive, there are important principles of management that have helped to create successful urban open spaces, and which can be highlighted simply. These are:

◆ Strategic approaches where local authorities have made a serious attempt to examine the management, finance, and distribution of different kinds of open space. These approaches quickly lead to the development of inter-disciplinary management teams, and to management plans that state objectives and link them clearly to expenditure.

◆ Strategies for parks are more likely to be effective if they reflect the core aims of the local authority. Where policies for parks have been considered as an integral part of corporate policy - to leisure, town centre management, to economic development, tourism, planning, pedestrian links as well as to environmental issues - this is reflected in better quality of park provision.

◆ Community involvement is often the key to successful open spaces. The best run community gardens and the poorest quality municipal parks are worlds apart. The belief in the value of community involvement and community consultation is universal, but its practice is much more limited. How far are local authorities really prepared to go? Should community groups manage their own budgets and take real decisions or are they simply puppets by which local authorities can prove their community credentials? How has effective community development been achieved?

Methodology

This report takes as its starting point the role parks can play in the regeneration of towns and cities. Whilst concentrating on 'urban parks', recognition is given to a range of other types of open space. Indeed urban parks are part of a wider continuum of public space and their role (and their management) cannot be divorced from more all embracing concepts of social and environmental regeneration, improving urban quality and enhancing city streets and squares.

In order to select the case-studies, a press release was issued at the beginning of August 1995, targeted at the appropriate professional and trade press in the horticultural, landscaping and local authority fields, appealing for examples of good practice. A number of the most widely circulated journals carried this appeal, as did the DoE and the AMA through their own newsletters circulated to all local authorities, urban development agencies and other related bodies. The principal researchers spoke about the good practice guide at several conferences, wrote to a number of individuals known to be widely knowledgeable about contemporary parks developments seeking their suggestions, and contacted a number of local authorities, trusts and professional bodies. Everything possible was done in the time available to widen the call for case-study material.

Many authorities were keen to co-operate, and it is their good practice on which this report is substantially based; and we are grateful to them. The process understandably has provided no guarantee of regional or political balance.

The Structure of this Report

Section 2 of the report is a synthesis of thirty-eight case-study examples grouped together under ten main themes which together provide a comprehensive survey of current urban parks management. There are twelve main case-studies, based on in-depth research, and a further twenty-six supplementary case-studies providing supporting evidence.

Theme	Summary of main issues
Planning:	The necessity for forward planning for parks provision, and the need for clear information as a precondition for effective management and decision-making.
Managing:	The role of multi-disciplinary management teams; current debates about the differing standards in 'indoor' and 'outdoor' leisure and the role for individual park management plans.
Competing:	The impact of the 1988 legislation requiring local authorities to put maintenance programmes out to competitive tender. It details both negative and positive effects of these changes.
Delegating:	The need to develop partnership funding for parks combined with the arrival of lottery funding, is leading to pressures for new organisational forms such as trusts. In this section three existing trusts which are managing urban parks are examined.
Maintaining:	The way in which standard and routine forms of maintenance need to be challenged, because 'greening strategies', as well as 'leisure strategies', require a more active and developmental approach. Maintaining means creating a robust park infrastructure and pleasant environment whilst being responsive to changing needs and demands.
Building:	The report challenges the convention that parks are always best kept as residual natural landscapes and suggests that they are often enhanced as places for activities by building-based provision.
Monitoring:	There is currently little evidence of the 'how, why, when and where' aspects of urban park use. It is suggested that parks should be seen as important leisure amenities and that monitoring use is essential if they are to win the case for funding as well as being able to respond to local need.
Involving:	The ways in which people with new skills can facilitate much greater community involvement in parks.
Funding:	New opportunities for funding particularly through urban regeneration programmes, partnership developments with environmental agencies, lottery money, as well as in the franchising of facilities within popular town parks.
Moving on:	The need to put parks provision within a wider corporate context, including developing relations with health, housing, education and environmental programmes.

The core text in Section 2 refers the reader to case-studies in Section 3 which illustrate the issues under discussion. A guide to the main themes covered by the case-studies is shown in Table 1. The case-studies provide further descriptive information and provide names and contact addresses and telephone numbers to allow the reader to follow up particular areas of interest.

Table 1 Case-study themes

Theme	Case-study	No
Buildings in parks	Cannon Hill Park, Birmingham	3.25
	Mid-Sussex	3.27
Children's play	Victoria Park, Ashford	3.1
	Stirling DC	3.11
	Victoria Park, Bath	3.13
	LB Lambeth	3.24
	Mid-Sussex DC	3.27
	North Herts DC	3.28
City centre renewal	Castle Park, Bristol	3.4
	Birmingham City Centre	3.16
	Castlefield Urban Heritage Park	3.21
Community development	Bristol City Council	3.2
	Rossmere Park, Hartlepool	3.5
	Walsall MBC	3.10
	Stirling DC	3.11
	Bromley-by-Bow	3.18
	Quaking Houses Community Garden	3.31
	St. George's Gardens, Camden	3.35
CCT contracts	Cheltenham BC	3.23
	Milton Keynes Parks Trust	3.8
	Oldham MBC	3.30
	LB Richmond	3.33
Controlling dogs	Calderdale	3.19
Disability access	Stirling DC	3.11
	North Hertforshire DC	3.28
Environmental education	LB Hounslow	3.6
	Centre of the Earth, Birmingham	3.22
Events	Battersea Park	3.14
	Cannon Hill Park, Birmingham	3.25
Full-time staff on site	West Ham Park	3.12
	Morden Hall	3.9
Health	Birmingham Health & Fitness Officer	3.32
	Stockport MBC	3.36
Income generation	Calderdale	3.19
	Morden Hall Park	3.9
Individual park management plans	Victoria Park, Ashford	3.1
	Battersea Park	3.14
	Walsall Arboretum	3.37
Infrastructure of facilities: parking/toilets/refreshments	Calderdale	3.19
	Cannon Hill Park, Birmingham	3.25
Linking indoor & outdoor leisure	Mid-Sussex DC	3.27
	Birmingham Health & Fitness Officer	3.32

Management by trusts	Milton Keynes	3.8
	Morden Hall Park	3.9
	Bromley-by-Bow	3.18
Multi-disciplinary teams	Victoria Park, Ashford	3.1
	LB Bromley	3.3
	Castle Park, Bristol	3.4
New skills	Birmingham Health & Fitness Officer	3.32
	Stockport MBC	3.36
	LB Southwark	3.34
	LB Merton	3.26
Partnership funding	Rossmere Park, Hartlepool	3.5
	National Urban Forestry Unit	3.17
	Urban Wildlife Groups	3.38
	Bromley-by-Bow	3.18
	Castlefield Heritage Park	3.21
Park strategies	LB Bromley	3.3
	LB Hounslow	3.6
	Bedford DC	3.15
	LB Newham	3.29
Tourism	Castle Park, Bristol	3.4
	Castlefield Urban Heritage Park	3.21
Urban regeneration	Hulme Regeneration	3.7
Volunteer involvement	Walsall MBC	3.10
	Morden Hall Park	3.9
	Urban Wildlife Groups	3.38
Value for money & monitoring	Victoria Park, Cardiff	3.20

The report concludes with a bibliography, together with a list of useful contacts and appropriate organisations.

Chapter 2. Summary of Good Practice

2.1 Planning:
the need for information-based strategies

Introduction

The story of the decline of public parks departments is widely known. Many things have changed since the days when the municipal parks service was the jewel in the local authority crown, commanding ranks of gardeners, skilled horticulturists and park-keepers, and when the Parks Superintendent stood side by side with the Lord Mayor to receive the town's visiting dignitaries. Recent decades of change - of radical local authority re-organisation, the emergence of a massive consumer leisure industry, loss of skilled staff, budget reductions culminating in the introduction of Compulsory Competitive Tendering (CCT) - have posed serious questions about the future of public parks.

The management response was to cut and make do, until the vestiges of the old model of horticultural excellence were unrecognisable in modern parks. And yet, the tenets of this earlier 'model of plenty' still informed the current bare-boned service. In most instances what was needed was a clear strategy to re-direct the parks service to meet the requirements of modern day cities, a plan to deliver the service within the new realities of local government and clear arguments to justify public parks as central to its concerns. Many authorities have begun to take such a strategic approach to parks provision.

Which department?

Most public parks in the UK are run by local authorities, and most are located in leisure services departments. In some places, parks provision has been re-defined as part of a corporate approach to environmental concerns, and parks services are located in an environmental directorate. Both have advantages and disadvantages, and each local authority will want to make its own priorities. Most important, however, is that parks provision is close to the core concerns of the authority, for, as was noted in the introduction, public parks are in many ways the testing-ground for the debate about urban sustainability.

Exploring new constituencies

In approaching the planning stage, it may be appropriate first to explore in depth the views of different sectors of the population surrounding the park in question. This may involve the use of focus groups and other interview techniques, as well as more quantitative market research methods or a community development approach. It may also call for more imaginative arts-based events or initiatives (such as music festivals, fairs) aimed at attracting interest in the potential local resource offered by a park. Lancashire County Council, for example, has used focus group methods to good effect in the context of planning its own Local Agenda 21 initiative.

Part of the wider vision

The parks strategy in Bromley, for example, is clearly positioned as part of the council's quest to become an enabling authority (CASE-STUDY 3). The parks service itself is seen as part of the broader project of social regeneration and the concern to make urban environments better places to live in. Newham's draft strategy sets out a role for the parks as a central part of the borough's plans for community development, and outlines the way in which the parks service can be fully incorporated within an environmental programme. The strategy rests on the establishment of a Parks Management Team. The aim is to put parks at the heart of the commitment to provide leisure services, and therefore the strategy argues that all those involved in leisure provision at a senior level should also be involved in the parks service (CASE-STUDY 29).

In Birmingham, the strategies for reinvestment in the city centre provided the context for the development of new city centre gardens (CASE-STUDY 16). The gardens are part of a wider programme to make the city centre more attractive for pedestrians. They are linked to a 'public realm network' which includes the new squares, canal-side walks and pedestrian routes and are included within the new city centre management programme. The new gardens are also a feature in the policy to support and enhance the residential areas around the city centre. The same is also true in Ashford, Kent, where the strategic position of Victoria Park in the identity and quality of the town centre is also now recognised, especially in the light of the impact of the new international passenger station (CASE-STUDY 1).

Mapping and counting

Creating inventories of the amount of open space for which the parks service is responsible, working out the costs of maintaining it, setting standards to direct the way it is to be maintained, and formulating a clear rationale for the provision of parks are the first steps towards developing a plan for the service as a whole. Many authorities have begun to

map their sites in detail, and most authorities have chosen paper systems while others have invested in computerised geographical information systems (GIS). The University of Greenwich Department of Architecture and Landscape is currently evaluating a colour-coded digital map system for the Borough of Greenwich. This system is intended to record some qualitative features of the landscape as well as the quantitative data. The process of drawing up inventories of work was a huge task; Bath's computerised inventory covers 10,000 sites and 60,000 tasks. For many authorities, the introduction of CCT meant that they began to map their parks, often for the first time, and many acknowledge the value of this exercise.

> 'The process has revolutionised our financial management. We know what everything costs - we can even compare costs per head for different parks.'
> PARKS MANAGER, EAST ANGLIA

It became clear that one of the weaknesses of direct maintenance had been the lack of supervision and monitoring. In the past, park managers were said to be bound by a rigid departmental structure in which financial management was carried out separately from the daily managerial responsibility of the parks. Managers were also said to lack good quality management information and were constrained by the inflexibility of grounds maintenance work practices. As a result, park management was effectively confined to the day-to-day supervision of grounds maintenance, other professional skills were often marginalised, and there was little scope for innovation.

These structural weaknesses were reproduced in early CCT contracts and contract management. There was an emphasis on the details of maintenance - how often the grass was cut, how near a tree a strimmer could be used - and not enough on meeting public concerns. Inputs rather than outcomes were stressed. Many authorities are now moving from measurement-based contracts to performance-based contracts. The shift from drawing up maintenance tasks to thinking more about outcomes and the overall performance of the service, together with information about the park sites and their costs, prepares the ground for a parks strategy.

What a strategy can deliver:

◆ A clear framework for all members of the local authority staff;

◆ A clear framework for partners, such as Friends Groups and sports clubs;

◆ A planned programme for investment (as opposed to financial fire-fighting);

◆ A clear statement of objectives, priorities and plans for park-users and potential partners;

◆ A re-connection between the objectives of the parks service and other major areas of local authority policy.

Developing the parks service

For most authorities, contracts have bedded down and park managers have been able to turn to questions of policy, quality of service, innovation and development. Many authorities are now developing strategic approaches to their parks service. The London Borough of Bromley's Parks and Open Spaces strategy has effected change both in the operational side of parks management and in the developmental side - parks as places that meet the leisure needs of the urban population. The strategy has been developed over the last three years and is applied to one part of the borough at a time. The Bromley strategy is based on the following elements:

◆ Re-classification of park types according to the different facilities they offer;

◆ An attempt to understand the needs and requirements of park-users;

◆ Re-configuration of expenditure to allow for directed investment;

◆ Change in organisational culture;

◆ Change in staff roles and the development of multi-disciplinary teams.

The strategy set the terms for measuring success and failure; it provided justification for the parks service and made a strong case for the service fulfilling the fundamental aim of the authority in its overriding concern to make Bromley a better place to live.

Park strategies are a way of making explicit the intentions and plans of the parks service and consulting with a wider audience of park-users. Bedford Borough Council published a Consultation Draft Parks Strategy for public debate in September 1994 (CASE-STUDY 15). The document is a clear and well written account of the policies the council wishes to pursue and on which it is seeking public comment. It is short, to the point, well designed and easily accessible. The strategy document sets out the philosophical approach taken by the council and details six proposed policies, each with an action plan, an estimate of the costs involved and a timetable. In January 1996 Glasgow City Council published 'A New Vision, A New Future', a comprehensive parks and open spaces strategy, covering parks, city centre civic spaces and areas on the urban fringe.

Understanding the use made of different types of parks

Until very recently parks were usually classified according to their size and their potential catchment area. Little attempt was made to assess the quality and distinctive features of different kinds of parks. The Bromley strategy team reviewed the types of open space they had - parks, gardens, recreation grounds, woodlands, country parks, circular walks, golf courses, allotments, and dual use facilities. They reviewed the GLC's Greater London Development Plan and the hierarchy of provision - metropolitan park, district park, local, and small local park. Whilst the GLDP approach had been successful in protecting public parks and open spaces from built development, the council felt it was no longer sufficient as a framework for developing parks and open space. They wanted a strategy that could take more account of the variety of parks and open spaces and the different uses made of them.

The borough carried out market research which showed that people made clear distinctions between sports grounds, formal gardens and the more general multi-purpose park providing a mix of facilities such as gardens, sports areas, cafés and children's playgrounds. The strategy proposed a new typology of green open space. A similar exercise has been carried out in Hounslow as part of the council's Green Strategy (CASE-STUDY 6). This strategy includes areas outside parks, such as green chain links, and knits them all together in a comprehensive environmental strategy.

Not just paper exercises

Strategies can very easily be paper exercises. The advantage of the phased approach taken by Bromley was that the staff team were able to pilot the strategy: the borough was divided into several areas and the strategy has been implemented in one area at a time. Crucially this has allowed for greater prioritisation of particular parks for more intensive management and it has allowed for the re-use of existing budgets to make fewer but more effective financial interventions within the parks service. It also meant that the borough could work out the strategy in practice and modify the process as it developed.

Financing a strategy

In past park management practice, financial management has often been tied to inflexible maintenance routines which do not allow much leeway to invest, vary or concentrate revenue expenditure. Bromley's decision to re-direct a proportion of existing revenue expenditure to pay for the pilot strategy was crucial to the project. It allowed for a critical re-assessment of the existing spending patterns. Instead of routinely spending revenue funds evenly across all the parks in the borough to little noticeable effect, the decision was made to concentrate spending so that more significant achievements could be made, but in fewer parks.

The fact that the strategy identified a clear programme of funding made it easier to specify the rationale for grant applications and to direct and demonstrate a positive use for external sources of money when they

became available. Council officers were able to demonstrate their plans to improve an area of park and show how additional funds could be channelled into the wider park improvement programme.

End of section checklist

- ◆ Is there an adequate inventory of parks and open spaces?
- ◆ Is there a strategy for parks and how does this relate to the wider corporate strategy?
- ◆ Is the current classification of parks and open spaces flexible enough to encompass all the types and uses?

2.2 Managing:

a multi-disciplinary approach integrating indoor and outdoor provision

Indoor and outdoor leisure

What such strategies seek to overcome are the current dual standards in much local authority leisure provision between indoor and outdoor leisure. This argument has been made forcefully in recent years by senior officers in Middlesbrough's leisure services team, who have rallied support to urban parks by describing them as 'leisure centres without a roof', seeking to secure for parks the same standards of customer service, support facilities such as catering and toilet provision, that indoor leisure provides. This is likely to develop as an important rationale for future parks provision, and is often referred to in this report, as local authorities elsewhere seek to re-integrate indoor and outdoor provision - especially in the wake of a recent succession of long hot summers when parks have been well used.

New management teams

Park management strategies can provide a framework within which to introduce a range of professional skills. Each park in the Bromley pilot strategy area was assigned a 'multi-disciplinary team'. Most teams had landscape designers, arboriculturists, parks patrol staff, countryside rangers, grounds maintenance staff, events staff and an ecologist. The teams for each particular site were selected to match the skills of the staff to the requirements of the park. The multi-disciplinary teams were considered to be particularly effective as they allowed for a mix of different expertise, and staff were able to understand their own roles within the development of the parks service as a whole.

Before multi-disciplinary teams were set up, different groups of staff worked according to their own professional perspectives and goals. Working as part of the team gave each member a clearer focus for their own work. More importantly, the strategy provided a longer term framework and so the sense of simply responding to each demand for

action was replaced by more coherent planning ahead. Staff teams allowed for a more creative approach, they boosted morale and provided a better sense of support and mutual encouragement.

Individual park management plans

Where local authorities feel in control of the overall management of their parks, they are now moving towards developing individual parks management plans. Clearly a park as large and multi-functional as Battersea Park (CASE-STUDY 14) requires a management plan of its own, and indeed an on-site management team, but even smaller public parks may best secure individual attention where the local authority works together with the community to decide more precisely what each park does best, and how this can be enhanced. A public space as historically unique as St George's Gardens in Camden, London (CASE-STUDY 35) has to be managed quite differently from any other of Camden's many parks and open spaces, and the development of the Friends of St George's Gardens is likely to provide an important forum for findings ways in which it might be managed appropriately.

Calderdale Council has set up a Park Management Group for Shibden Park in Halifax, involving parks officers, a tourism officer, and representatives of the several franchisees who operate there, as a means of working together to promote the park, and to ensure that all public and commercial facilities in the park complement each other (CASE-STUDY 19).

An individual park management plan might include:

◆ A declaration of aims for the park and ambitions for its future, on the part of the authority, and partners such as local groups;

◆ A statement summarising appraisals of the park, including assessments of use, access, circulation, physical analysis, ecological analysis and visual analysis;

◆ An action plan stating agreed priorities, areas for investment and a development schedule for a specified time-frame (eg 3 years, 5 years);

◆ A design concept for the different areas of the park (formal, wild, water, informal, sports, play, dog management) and a tailor-made maintenance programme and financial plan to support it;

◆ A financial plan outlining current expenditure and income, for the park as a whole and then for elements within it (eg staffing, contracts, built facilities, sports facilities, security, vandalism repairs, etc) and projected changes;

◆ A statement of how park management at all levels will operate (managers, rangers, security staff, temporary staff such as play workers as well as contractors);

◆ A clear statement of the role of partners, such as Friends Groups, wildlife groups, sports clubs, one o'clock clubs, facilities operating under franchise, delegated management or stewardship arrangements, and statements from each about how they would like to develop;

◆ An events programme, including opportunities for voluntary groups to run their own events;

◆ A framework for encouraging wider community participation, for example schools;

◆ An intention to review the implementation of the management plan, to set targets and to measure progress.

A management plan should provide a clear framework that unites all involved in the park from voluntary groups to contractors, but it should also remain flexible, able to respond to unexpected events and ideas, and open to new partners. It should be a clear guide to support park management, not a manual that restricts it.

Self-management and delegated management

A number of local authorities are moving towards greater involvement of local communities in the management of parks (see later section on *Involving* also). In Calderdale, Wellholme Park is one of 19 parks now managed by a local community group under the council's self-management programme. The majority of these sites have bowling clubs which have been the focus for developing greater community involvement in the management of the parks, and their remit now extends to running facilities such as tennis courts, playgrounds, and pitch and putt greens. Although there have been some problems in securing long-term community involvement in some areas of Calderdale, in general the scheme has been a great success.

The delegated management of certain kinds of public open spaces is quite a long tradition: many allotments around Britain have often been managed by the allotment-holders themselves, under agreements drawn up with the local authority. Increasingly bowling greens and club-houses are now directly managed by the clubs themselves, who often provide additional funds for improvements and even paid staffing.

End of section checklist

◆ *Do the same standards apply to both indoor and outdoor provision for leisure?*

◆ *Are all the professional skills in place to develop the strategy?*

◆ *Do the larger parks within the portfolio have their own individual management plans?*

◆ *What aspects of park management are amenable to delegated or community self-management?*

2.3 Competing:
integrating management and maintenance

By 1 January 1994, nearly all ground maintenance work paid for by local authorities was
subject to competitive tender, under the
Local Government Act 1988. The Audit
Commission report, "Competitive Management of Parks & Green Spaces", estimated
that this would produce savings of 10-30%,
though it accepted that there might be some
off-setting increases in expenditure, notably
annual administration costs of about 4% of
the annual contract sum. However, it argued
that good authorities would already be
spending this sort of sum in supervising their
own workforce, although it later emerged
that one of the weaknesses of direct maintenance had been a lack of supervision and
monitoring. It was expected that CCT would
produce dramatic effects, including new
forms of management and maintenance,
which are being felt throughout parks
services everywhere.

According to the Audit Commission, in order
to prepare for CCT, local authorities were
advised to:

◆ Set out an area by area policy on parks
  provision and use;

◆ Review and document maintenance
  standards required;

◆ Establish new management structures
  with clear roles for committees, officers
  and distinctions between client and
  contractor functions;

◆ Establish an inventory of work to be
  done;

◆ Divide the work so as to produce the
  most competitive bids;

◆ Specify requirements relating to tasks and
  standards of performance;

◆ Install appropriate inspection
  arrangements;

◆ Plan not only how to monitor contractor
  performance, but also 'how they will
  check that facilities continue to be used
  by those for whom they are intended'.

Most of this was a straightforward
management task, but the first and last
requirements were more interesting. They
stated that a detailed parks policy was
required by each local authority, and that
ensuring continuing use by the public was a
central objective. The use of parks and
providing a better service to the public were
therefore at least as important as any
financial saving which might be made.

Contracts

According to several direct services
organisations (DSOs) managers, the biggest
problem to date has been the poor quality of
contract specification. In the client-contractor
split, the more entrepreneurial officers often
went into the DSO, leaving others to draw
up contracts. Early ones were often cribbed,
it is said, from those drawn up by other
authorities, and weaknesses compounded.
The London Borough of Richmond's contract
for nature conservation work was quite
different, because real efforts were made to
consult effectively with local people about its
implications (CASE-STUDY 33). As a result it
had to be made more comprehensible, and a
guide to the contracting documents was also
prepared. Each section begins with a brief
vision for the area in question.

The main problems which the early days of
CCT brought to light included:

◆ Adoption of standardised specifications
  (often borrowed from other authorities),
  which were not necessarily appropriate to
  local conditions;

◆ An over-emphasis on details of inputs,
  rather than public outcomes;

◆ Inflexibility of interpretation - if it wasn't
  in the contract, then it wouldn't get done,
  however necessary;

◆ Adversarial relations between client and
  contractor, at times, even if both
  belonged to same local authority;

- Past maintenance regimes, not always the best, rigidified and codified into contract specifications;
- Little attention given to management issues, and public consultation.

However, a second generation of contracts has gained much from this early experience, and managers are now more confident in dealing with the contracting process.

Financial management

Most managers appreciate the greater clarity of the new financial arrangements. 'We now know what we have got and how much it costs to maintain it,' said one officer. The downside is that enhancements which were once disguised within overall management budgets are now conspicuous, with the result that they may be judged too expensive. There is also a temptation to keep 'profitable' activities undertaken by a DSO in order to help them make up their rate of return, even if the operation itself is no longer required for policy reasons. A parks manager in the West Midlands certainly thought that budgetary controls needed to be improved, even though there was much better sense of what was happening.

Savings and their destination

Research on the introduction of CCT by Walsh and Davis from the Institute of Local Government Studies at Birmingham University 'Competition and Service: The Impact of the Local Government Act 1988' (HMSO 1993) found savings of 7% across all services and of 11% in grounds maintenance. This is after taking account of the costs of the client side.

Later research on a different sample of local authorities by Bill Swan of the University of Reading, the summary findings of which were published in Horticulture Week detailed below, found that authorities had made savings averaging 16% as a result of CCT, but that in less than a third of cases was any of the money saved made available to the parks service.

The redirection of maintenance savings to parks development work 1994	
Authorities using all savings for parks development	4%
Authorities using some savings for parks development	30%
Authorities using no savings for parks development	66%

(Source : Horticulture Week, 19 January 1995)

Many departments reported that savings produced by CCT were soaked up by contracts management and monitoring costs. In 200 audits reported on in ' Making Markets: A Review of the Audits of the Client Role for Contracted Services', 1995 the Audit Commission found considerable variation in client-side costs and recommended that even in small authorities, these costs could often be reduced without loss of control. Streamlining contract administration through output-based specifications, involving contractors and consumers in contract monitoring, and resolving problems at local level were some of the suggestions made.

In the past five years, Oldham's gardening staff has been reduced from 260 to 151, and at least £1 million lost from its parks maintenance budget. Yet the response from the public is that the parks are starting to look better than they have for a long time (CASE-STUDY 30). Although reluctant to criticise earlier managers, new staff in one authority did regret what might have been achieved if current management practice had been applied to earlier levels of funding and staff.

Financial arrangements under CCT are now much more transparent, with the following effects:

- It is now much clearer how much each park costs to manage and maintain;
- Identifying costs has made park 'luxuries' such as ornamental bedding, vulnerable to cuts;
- Savings have been made on maintenance costs but not necessarily returned to park budgets;

♦ Many local authorities have not yet found a workable balance between direct and contracted-out work, and small and large contracts.

How competitive is CCT?

Where there is limited interest in contracting for services, there is no guarantee that competitive advantage will be secured. The Local Government Management Board's regular national survey of CCT contracts, as reported in 'CCT information Service Survey Report, No 12' December 1995, shows that overall there is now significant competition for grounds maintenance contracts. On average, authorities invite seven contractors to bid and receive four tenders. Only 6.7% of current contracts have been won without competition. Reservations have been expressed by at least one authority to the effect that the disappearance of DSOs could in future result in less competition.

The Audit Commission's review of the client-side role judged that only 30% of authorities were 'positive' in generating contractor interest and encouraging bids for contracts. A dialogue with all potential tenderers, and the packaging of contracts to encourage bids (at various levels of potential expertise or capacity, including community-based environmental groups) is a critical part of the client role.

CCT can produce flexibility

An advantage of CCT is that parks managers are no longer constrained by limitations of in-house skills and equipment. They are much freer now to define and cost their objectives and find ways of achieving them. Cheltenham and Oldham DSOs have core teams which are supplemented as necessary by casual labour, particularly during the summer. One parks manager cited in the Horticulture Week feature on CCT said that, 'CCT has made it slower to introduce change and in this sense is less flexible. However, the changes which can be made are more profound and it is this, in the medium term, which allows more flexibility.'

Direct service organisations

A number of new organisations have been created to replace traditional DSOs, ranging from private limited companies, to structures which more or less imitate previous departmental responsibilities. Between these is the 'Super-DSO' which combines all functions (e.g. grounds maintenance, cleansing, building repairs etc.) into one body. DSOs were required by law to make a minimum 6% profit (or rate of return) on their contracts.

A majority of contracts to date have been won by the DSOs which were established as a result of the client/contractor split. Some councils have viewed the maintenance of a large workforce as a key means of influencing the local economy and labour market, and have prioritised supporting their DSOs as a result. This could be construed as an essentially reactive step, in other words, finding ways of safeguarding existing jobs. Other authorities have taken the more ambitious step of using their DSOs to bid for contracts outside their own services in other public services -Cheltenham DSO is an example (CASE STUDY 23). Glasgow DSO also handles contracts for the Scottish Office and the Scottish Development Agency. Many DSOs contacted in the study have lost staff in significant numbers, though most did not have exact figures to hand. An approximation would be reductions in the order of 25% of the original workforce. Glasgow now has between 1,700 and 1,800 people in its DSO, but had another 600 in the past. At the end of 1995 Birmingham Council's DSO failed to win the major city contract with massive repercussions within the local authority. It is the loss of 'static' staff in parks, permanent on-site gardeners and park-keepers, which has had the greatest impact on the public, as many park user surveys suggest. Some authorities are seeking to re-establish site-based maintenance as part of new contract specifications in order to reassure the public and to seek to reduce vandalism.

DSOs and quality

There is a split between those authorities who have taken the certification route, and those which have not. Glasgow has secured ISO 9002 (BS 5750, Part 2) for the whole DSO, and several have BS 5750. Hertfordshire County Council secured certification for the highways and ground maintenance operations. In other authorities, the Charter Mark plays a similar though less formal function. Cheltenham has not followed the ISO 9002 route, preferring instead to build quality through 'teamwork, openness and good management'. Oldham DSO secured BS 5750 in 1991, and the client side has seen this as an important factor in the success of their relationship, since it guarantees a certain level of quality, enabling the contract managers to step back a little and look at wider issues. They now depend on a good relationship with the DSO and BS 5750 to take care of everyday management problems, freeing up client-side officers to work with local people. The Royal Borough of Kensington & Chelsea is among a number of authorities seeking ISO 9002 accreditation for their client-side management of parks. Yet there may be some tensions between the effects of CCT, as currently implemented, and the wider pursuit of quality management, particularly where the latter involves employment security, employee development, and job satisfaction, and in which the ability of the local authority to influence these issues weakens through the contracting-out process. Even where contractors have accredited 'quality' management systems, management efficiency alone does not necessarily result in what the public regard as improved standards or provision in the Parks themselves.

Improving quality

Derby City Council has split its contracts between a DSO (60%) and two private contractors. The parks manager supports this and thinks that the comparison is useful: each supervisor works with both the DSO and a private contractor, so that they are able to make comparisons and draw ideas across. The parks in Kensington & Chelsea (including Holland Park) are maintained and managed by a private company called Serco Ltd on a £1.3 million contract. Serco won the contract again for 4-6 years in 1994. This dual management and maintenance contract is at present quite rare, but re-integrating management and maintenance, whether in-house or as an external contract, is likely to find favour again in future.

The research by Bill Swan cited earlier also found some agreement that the CCT process had helped with quality, partly by defining it, but argued that quality was more consistently achieved in playing fields than in parks. In Ipswich it was thought that overall, quality had not changed - though quality is becoming increasingly important - but that it had become more standardised, whereas in the past, there could be greater variation depending on local teams. In Kensington & Chelsea, Glasgow, Ettrick and Lauderdale, Hull and elsewhere, the view was also that quality had been maintained or improved, yet elsewhere doubts continue. CCT has clearly produced different effects in different places.

Monitoring and enforcement

People contacted, on both sides of the client-contractor divide, generally expressed satisfaction with the way that the two halves co-operate.

> 'I can't remember the last time we had to pick up the specification to argue about something - it must be three years ago now.'
> PARKS MANAGER, NORTH WEST

About 25% of local authorities claim to be experiencing difficulties with monitoring contractors' work and enforcing contractual compliance. The reason commonly given was inadequate staffing. It is suggested that the move from frequency (input) to performance (output) based monitoring will ease the strain.

Managing parks

Several DSO managers interviewed would like contracts to be extended to cover the whole management of a park, not just its maintenance, as with the Holland Park example. Their teams had the skills and expertise to do it, and 'there's lots of things we'd like to do to enhance the parks'. But others are very clear that the way CCT has been implemented by some authorities appeared to separate maintenance from management and development functions.

> *'At first, everybody was too concerned with managing contracts, to manage parks.'*
> PARKS MANAGER, NORTH WEST

Ironically, CCT legislation did not prevent local authorities from putting more than maintenance out to contract. If they had put it all out, they would almost certainly have prevented many contracts going to the private sector, since in the early days of CCT private sector expertise often did not extend beyond maintenance. Oldham MBC have a very positive view of the way that CCT had enabled managers to begin to manage the parks: 'We've been able to take our eyes up from the maintenance problems and get back to managing the parks', a sentiment echoed by officers at the Milton Keynes Parks Trust (CASE-STUDY 8).

The lessons of CCT

The introduction of CCT signalled a radical change in the way in which local authority parks are today managed and maintained; there have been healthy improvements and some problems.

Improvements

- The need to produce inventories of local public open space, and in many cases to literally map them, has been a great step forward, in terms of thinking strategically about provision. For a number of local authorities this was the first time they had been required to produce an audit of the open space within their responsibility.
- The need to draw up maintenance contracts in itself required that parks managers had to start thinking seriously about what each park was for and how best it could be maintained to achieve that purpose, a crucial issue dealt with in

several other sections of this report. This process of critical thinking about purpose is still in its infancy.

- The introduction of CCT has generated greater public debate about what parks are for and how they are best managed. Parks funding is now a matter of local controversy rather than mute acceptance of slow decline.
- CCT has required that the costs of maintaining and managing parks are becoming more transparent (as 'cost centres') - and therefore public. Knowing that a neighbourhood park costs so much money to maintain is beginning to lead some community groups to say 'we could do that', and in some cases this might be a better option.
- Savings have been achieved through the impact of competition (although not always returned to the overall parks budget).

Drawbacks

- In some cases CCT has led to a split between management, maintenance and security. Everything has focused on the maintenance contract and savings to be effected there, while failing to acknowledge the public's deep reservations about tidier parks being achieved at the expense of staffing and safety.
- The visible loss of 'static' or site-based park staff has been linked, by a number of local authorities and community groups, to a rise in vandalism.
- The tendency to package parks maintenance contracts in large parcels to suit the needs of competitive tendering, can mean that the possibility of small, community-based management and maintenance proposals for local parks is not considered.

End of section checklist

- *Does the CCT process enhance the relationship between maintenance and management?*
- *Does the tendering process allow a variety of bidders to compete?*

2.4 Delegating:

partnerships, self-management and trusts

For a variety of reasons, there are individual parks or collections of parks in Britain not owned or managed by local authorities, most notably the Royal Parks, National Trust parks, the Milton Keynes Parks Trust, and a small number of parks in London owned and managed by the Corporation of London. For the purposes of this study we looked at the funding and management regimes of three of these bodies, as they pertained to parks in urban areas, notably the Milton Keynes Parks Trust (CASE-STUDY 8), the National Trust management of Morden Hall Park in the London Borough of Merton (CASE-STUDY 9), and the Corporation of London's management of West Ham Park in the London Borough of Newham (CASE-STUDY 12). The purpose was to see what could be learned from the experience of funding and managing urban parks by autonomous, usually specialist bodies. (The three examples summarised below are described at greater length in the Case-Studies)

The Milton Keynes Parks Trust

The Milton Keynes Parks Trust was established in 1992 to take over the funding and management of many of the town's parks and open spaces from the Milton Keynes Development Corporation. There had been some discussion as to whether the parks should be handed over to the local authority with an endowment, as had been the common practice in erstwhile new towns. However, it was finally agreed to hand the freehold over to the Borough Council whilst setting up the charitable trust to take responsibility for operating the parks on a long lease. The Board of the Trust contains a mixture of nominated members representing many of the main interest groups which would naturally have an interest in the quality and management of local green open space, including the Buckinghamshire, Berkshire and Oxfordshire Naturalist Trust, the Royal Forestry Society, the Royal Agricultural Society, three

nominations from the local authority, from the parish councils, from the local Chamber of Commerce and the local Sports Council. All Board members must live or work in Milton Keynes, and are subject to re-nomination or replacement every three years.

The work of the Trust is funded out of income generated by a property portfolio which was given to the Trust on its incorporation. This covers the cost of managing and maintaining the Trust's 4,000 acres of parkland and the commercial property portfolio. The Trust employs some twenty staff including secretarial, administrative, rangers, landscape officers, with a senior management team made up of the Landscape & Forestry Manager, the Parks & Estates Manager, the Finance & Administrative Manager and the Chief Executive. The Trust operates from a purpose-built headquarters in Campbell Park.

Accountability

The Milton Keynes Parks Trust is conscious of a need to demonstrate local 'accountability', given that it is not part of the elected local authority structure, and it would claim to do this through close contact with the public through the ranger service, and through undertaking regular visitor research, which is then used to inform policy. The Trust has recently decided to establish a network of focus groups in Milton Keynes to provide additional information and act as a sounding board for local opinion, with regard to park provision.

It is clear that parks provision in Milton Keynes benefits from having a dedicated agency working solely to a single remit, without having constantly to fight political battles for resources with other, equally important, local services, or follow the occasional vagaries of national and local political decision-making. Yet ironically, a majority of Milton Keynes park-users are unaware that the parks are run by a Trust and assume them to be just another local authority service. Equally interesting is the lack of concern by Trust staff that this is the case, for as one of them stated:

> 'We are not over-worried about whether the public knows it is us that run the parks or the local council; the important thing is that the customers think that the parks are run well, and enjoy using them.'
>
> SENIOR OFFICER,
> MILTON KEYNES PARKS TRUST

Morden Hall Park

Morden Hall Park in South London, has been owned and run by the National Trust since 1941. The 125 acre estate is a mix of meadowland, old marshland, woodland and more formal garden areas. Over the last five years the Trust has combined its conservation aims with the successful development of the park. Unlike many other National Trust sites, they do not charge for entry to the park as the donor had requested that the park should be accessible to the public free of charge. The Trust had to find other ways of raising income to help support the management and maintenance costs of the park.

In the early 1990s the nursery buildings within the walled garden became vacant. The Trust approached several garden centre companies and asked for proposals for investing in the site. The arrangement finally agreed with a garden centre company involved:

◆ An investment by the company in the site to build the garden centre and to carry out a programme of restoration;

◆ The building of the shell of the café and shop (the interior was fitted out by the Trust);

◆ The provision and maintenance of the car park;

◆ Maintaining the historic nursery garden walls.

In return the company were awarded a long lease. The development of the garden centre and café created the momentum for the restoration of the park. The buildings provided a focal point for people and for further activity as well as supplying regular income for the park. They have also paved the way for re-establishing a use for Morden Hall itself.

Trust status

Morden Hall Park has special trust status allowing surplus operating income to be spent directly on projects in Morden Hall Park. The park is able to raise income from the rental of property and leasehold:

◆ Registry Office, London Borough of Merton (rent);

◆ Private houses (rented out at market rates);

◆ Garden centre (annual contribution);

◆ Café and shop National Trust Enterprise Unit (all profit);

◆ Craft businesses (rent);

◆ Grazing paddocks (rent).

Staffing

The park is managed by the head warden and two full-time wardens. The three staff live on site. The presence of full-time staff on site is central to the overall success of the park. The head warden is a clear point of contact for individuals and groups who wish to find out more about the park. He has responsibility for the site as a whole, including property management (private and business rentals), educational activity, volunteer input, conservation and land management as well as security and overseeing general park use.

The mix of land conservation with the development, in partnership, of public, private and independent facilities (garden centre, café, city farm) has worked to create a thriving site bringing more people into the park.

The key elements of Morden Hall Park are:

◆ A manager and staff on site at all times;

◆ The management of the site as a whole (including buildings, education, craft workshops);

- Financial control and the capacity to generate income for the park;

- The synergy created between the different businesses in the park (they are interdependent);

- The clarity of vision or rationale for the park;

- The involvement of volunteers;

- The link with local history groups, conservation groups and local business;

- The good reputation of the Trust itself and its insistence on high standards.

West Ham Park

West Ham Park in the London Borough of Newham occupies seventy-seven acres and offers a number of facilities to its visitors: extensive open stretches of grass containing two football and two cricket pitches, nine tennis courts, a flower-crammed ornamental garden and large and well-equipped playground complete with paddling pool. It is very well used and popular with local people, who regard it as very well maintained and very safe.

West Ham Park is a City of London park. Its cousins are not Newham's local parks such as Plashet Park or West Ham Recreation Ground but Hampstead Heath, Highgate Woods and Epping Forest, all of which are also administered by the Corporation of London. What difference does it make, if any? The first and obvious answer is that West Ham Park has access to far more money that any borough park.

Money for staffing

West Ham's funds are undoubtedly generous, in present-day terms. The park's net expenditure for 1995/6 is £718,700, just under half of Newham borough's total parks budget which has to cover every bit of public-owned green space in the borough, quite apart from its 22 parks. It is both the quality and quantity of its staffing that gives West Ham an advantage. In all, the Corporation of London employs 16 park-keepers and gardeners, and there are up to 5 keepers on duty at any one time. Many have been employed for a number of

years, bringing continuity. At times of maximum usage, they are augmented by relief staff and members of an outside security firm. The staffing level has been raised because of the perception of the decline of borough parks, and management's fear that 'unruly elements' would spill over.

The money for West Ham Park comes not from local rates and taxes but from an ancient property fund, administered by a Management Committee with no local accountability. Critics will point to a total divorce from the feelings and affairs of local people and cite examples of park practice in support of their case. There is, for instance, no policy of allowing local groups to use the park for fetes, fairs or fund-raising events.

Yet West Ham Park is a great asset to its neighbourhood, and proves that money does matter, and that an abundance of dedicated site-based staffing can win loyalties, even when the providing organisation is relatively remote and uninvolved in the rest of the life of the community.

Are trusts the answer?

It is now widely accepted that unless local communities feel a sense of 'ownership' of local parks and open spaces, then vandalism may be a problem. Developments in delegated management and self-management appear to be ideas whose time has come, creating an active role for users and residents to be involved in park management and providing new sources of voluntary help, and funds, which parks need desperately in many places. But some would argue that there is a need to go further, and that where local authorities have failed to manage or maintain parks successfully, such parks should be managed and maintained by some form of trust. Not only would trusts offer opportunities for additional fund-raising, but could also provide more amenable and locally-based forms of management. It is also likely that the prospect of lottery funding may increase the pressures to manage more urban parks as trusts.

The overwhelming benefit which appears to derive from the ownership, management and funding of parks by a dedicated trust or organisation is the continuity of staff, the single-mindedness of the organisational ethos, the ability to raise outside funds, and the close attention to the job in hand. In addition, budgets are usually more secure, with savings re-invested in the parks themselves, rather than being siphoned off to other areas of need. Trusts can engender greater voluntary involvement, and find it easier to raise other sources of revenue.

While the experience of the trusts is invaluable, the issues facing parks departments in hundreds of local authorities are usually of a different scale and order, and will require different kinds of solutions. There are to date almost no examples of local authority parks being bequeathed into trust ownership - exceptions to this general pattern would include Bromley-by-Bow (CASE-STUDY 18) and the Hillsborough Memorial Park Trust, where one small corner of a traditional park has been taken into trust management in order to create a memorial park to the victims of the Hillsborough football disaster- but these are fairly unusual circumstances and are not likely to prove a solution to the problems facing the vast majority of urban parks.

Endowment trusts

The parks in Milton Keynes are managed by an endowment trust, which meets the costs of maintaining and managing the parks portfolio from the annual income received from a gift of property made by the Milton Keynes Development Corporation on its dissolution. This is a rare occurrence. Similarly the Corporation of London parks are also funded by historic endowment funds, complemented by provisions from one of the richest corporations in Britain. Morden Hall Park has to earn its annual keep through rents and franchises based on a unique portfolio of historic buildings. These circumstances are rare, and cannot be emulated by most local authorities as a means of funding local parks.

Other trusts

However, the future is likely to see a number of new kinds of urban green open space developed by independent organisations, whether voluntary organisations or trusts, which will complement existing local authority provision. For example, there are now 69 city farms in the UK which have between them reclaimed 550 acres of derelict urban land. The farms range in size from 91 acres to less than 0.1 acre, and receive more than 3 million visits a year, particularly by schoolchildren. City farms operate as self-financing independent community projects managed by locally elected management committees, and have to generate their own income through sponsorship, business grants, sales of produce, and so on. Most of them also receive grants from local authorities, and in most cases there is a good relationship with the local authority. The city farms have their own national organisation. City farms are just one example of a new kind of urban green space invariably developed by enthusiastic volunteers, and often operating as a trust. Such spaces complement traditional parks provision rather than compete with it.

It is anticipated that as more and more public housing is devolved to trust management, or as new social housing is created by housing associations or Housing Action Trusts, there will also be pressures to manage the open space in and around the housing more successfully than has generally been done in the past; indeed housing associations may well be moving into open space management, having already moved into job creation projects and youth work in some places.

Partnership

It is likely that local authorities will in future work more in partnership with independent environmental organisations and trusts. For example, Burgess Park in Southwark is being re-developed through a partnership between Southwark Council and Groundwork Southwark (one of a number of autonomous Groundwork trusts). The scale of the enterprise, one of the biggest new park developments in any European capital city and needing to raise £30 million, is of an order that would be difficult for a local authority alone to tackle, particularly an inner city borough with many other problems to be solved. As the Quaking Houses (Durham) case-study shows (CASE-STUDY 31), in other parts of the UK, regional and local sections of the Groundwork Trust are working with local authorities on dozens of partnership schemes.

End of section checklist

◆ Are there parks or park networks which would benefit from independent management?

◆ Is the park authority open to partnership with independent organisations and trusts?

2.5 Maintaining:

meeting new demands for flexible and robust spaces

Maintaining or developing?

As has already been noted, to date most CCT contracts have concentrated on maintenance specifications, often at the expense of wider management objectives. As the 1988 Audit Commission report said, 'too often parks are regarded as a legacy to be maintained rather than as an asset to be developed'. In the case-study on the impact of CCT, one parks manager thought that the contract specifications drawn up by his local authority 'read more like an idiot's guide to gardening, than a grounds maintenance contract.'

Yet maintenance is, of course, vital. It is what the public notices most when they enter a park: whether the railings, paths, flower-beds and areas of shrubbery are kept clean and in good repair, tidy and relatively weed-free, or whether they look neglected and unkempt. Good park maintenance is actually a pre-condition of the public's sense of security and trust.

There is much evidence to suggest that at least part of the current crisis in public parks is attributable to an imbalance between maintenance - which freezes development - and management - involving change. The historical dominance of horticulture in parks management, with an emphasis too often confined to bedding displays, has been a factor in limiting change, although some horticulturists have emerged as outstanding managers.

Successful and sustainable management demands a regime which manages change on two distinct levels:

◆ Activities taking place in the park;

◆ Physical changes which keep the park fit for the next activity due to take place.

This should not be construed as an argument in favour of perpetual, frenetic restructuring of the park to suit each day's new event: robustness is an essential quality in the design of parks in order that they can accommodate diverse activities. However, a park should be seen as a resource, to be moulded and fashioned over time in response to changes in patterns of life and composition of its potential users. An organisation is needed to detect those changing demands early and perform all the necessary fund-raising and implementation procedures in time for it to be of use. Such an organisation needs all the freedom it can get to assemble the necessary resources and apply them efficiently and single-mindedly. Recent constraints on public spending at central and local levels, and restrictions on funding arrangements, have affected the ability of councils to pursue these goals.

But there are also great - and perhaps increasing - problems of changing expectations on both sides as to what parks are for. For many people the local park, 'our park', is the one constant in a local landscape that has often been subject to massive changes. Around it buildings have come and gone, new roads have been cut through, the social and ethnic mix of the population has changed, yet the park has seemed to have been preserved as some timeless secret garden. For older people this is a source of continuity and comfort, and they want the park to be maintained as it always was. However, for parents with young children, or for local environmentalists, or for local authority officers who have been commissioned to draw up 'greening' strategies or Local Agenda 21 policies for parks, or for politicians who have to make yet again more financial cuts, the local park has to be able to meet changing circumstances.

Going green

Hence the need for strategies, and for forms of public consultation which arrive at an agreement as to what the local park is for and how it can be managed and maintained to achieve its new objectives. It is quite clear that where changes have taken place with little public consultation, there have been problems. The sudden decision to allow a section of a park to revert to a more natural 'wildlife area', allowing the grass to grow and all kinds of wild grasses and saplings to flourish, may to the public simply appear to be a policy of total neglect. This is less of a problem where a wildlife area of a public park is now managed by a voluntary group, who are often able to generate support and interest in their work through local connections.

On the other hand quite different horticultural policies have been pursued with little public consultation, though with greater short-term public approval. There is a debate to be had as to whether the diversion of resources in some local authorities, away from neighbourhood parks and towards 'Britain in Bloom' projects and schemes has long-term or environmental benefits. Certainly the 'Britain in Bloom' campaign has been a great success in making many town and city centres more attractive, in securing private sector involvement, and has had tourism and civic pride benefits. But when these are achieved at the expense of neighbourhood facilities, or local environmental distinctiveness, there is a need for greater public debate. It is also yet another shift - in this case with regard to horticultural display - away from the public park and to the town centre as a focus for public activity and civic vitality.

Hounslow's Green Strategy

To meet many of these changing demands, and involve the public in understanding the way ecological thinking is affecting public open space, Hounslow Council have developed a 'Green Strategy'. A key element of the strategy is nature conservation, but generally a broad approach to landscape and outdoor recreation was adopted in order to solve some of the problems of existing parks management, and to provide a more cost-effective approach to landscape maintenance and management through redesign.

Within the broader strategy each of the borough's 50 parks is to be assessed in

respect of a range of criteria including location, current use, individual landscape elements, historical connections, nature conservation interest, current maintenance methods and cost-effectiveness. After a period of public consultation, costed 'Masterplans' are then to be developed for each park. It is hoped that this process will allow the public to be involved in deciding upon and understanding how their local park is to be maintained in future, balancing patterns of use and need with a wider concern for ecology and environmental sustainability.

Parks within parks

Elsewhere wildlife areas have been developed in a number of local authority parks which are maintained by independent groups. One such example is in Holland Park in the Royal Borough of Kensington & Chelsea, where a wildlife enclosure was created in 1991, and where a project was undertaken in 1994 to improve the area and create greater educational links, with sponsorship coming from English Nature, London Electricity plc and the Friends of Holland Park. In 1995 moorhens started nesting in the site for the first time, and sparrowhawks and tawny owls are now regular visitors. The project also resulted in the creation of a community conservation group which takes responsibility for maintaining the pond and wildlife area, a pattern now widespread in local parks in the UK.

The basic infrastructure

Many parks are now competing for users within a much more commercialised or 'consumer' leisure market-place. Reference has been made elsewhere to the importance of integrating indoor and outdoor leisure policies. As the Park Life report revealed, what people want and expect from the 'family' or mixed activity park, is what they would expect from any other form of leisure provision: decent toilets, refreshments, well-maintained play equipment (since accompanying children remains the single most common reason given for visiting parks in all surveys), and at least some minimal form of 'customer care'.

Unless local authorities find ways of providing this basic infrastructure to selected or targeted parks within their responsibility, then they will have failed in serious measure. People will go elsewhere. The parks self-management programme of Calderdale Council, the successful development of Pallister Park in Middlesbrough as a 'leisure centre without a roof', and many other successful public parks, have all shown that these facilities can be provided and maintained, and as a result bring more users and more families, who stay for longer.

Access for all

There are also issues of developing an appropriate infrastructure for people with disabilities - a significant section of the population which the Park Life report research suggested was under-represented in park use - which means ensuring that access gates, paths, and park facilities are accessible to disabled people. Having done this, it is also important that disabled people are informed of these improvements and welcomed into the parks.

Newham's Community Parks Development Officer has a brief to work with local disability groups to facilitate better access and use of the parks by disabled people. As the Stirling and North Herts case-studies show, consultation with local communities about play facilities often brings to the fore the demand for integrated play provision (SEE CASE-STUDIES 11 & 28). Similarly, Charlton Park in Greenwich also has an integrated play area, adjacent to a riding school for the disabled, providing one of the most well-used features of the park.

Elderly people are often reluctant to use parks for reasons of safety. An exemplary pocket park development in Wellington by Wrekin Council, the Oak & Acorn Garden, was based on developing a piece of waste ground which separated a school from a small estate of sheltered housing for the elderly into a shared facility. The land has been landscaped to produce ponds and

wetlands linked by walkways and bridges, and sheltered seating and attractive planting have been provided for the elderly. It is popular with everybody.

Design and manage

Where parks have been re-designed, refurbished, or even created new, it is now felt to be a matter of priority that landscape design should not be regarded as a once-and-for-all commission, but should be managed appropriately as a long-term process. This is certainly the view of the Landscape Institute who have argued that 'unlike the case in many European and North American countries, landscape architects are woefully under-represented in the management of urban parks in Britain. This belies the fact that design and management of the growth of any landscape is a continuous and iterative process'. The Hounslow Green Strategy is being undertaken by the Landscaping and Environmental Services department of Hounslow Council, and in Wrekin and Ashford, landscape management also plays a prominent role within a local authority departmental structure.

Dealing with vandalism

All parks suffer vandalism to a greater or lesser degree, and it is an essential part of the maintenance programme to deal with it. The lessons from the Calderdale and Hartlepool case-studies point to the need to tackle vandalism as a priority, and to stay ahead of the game. In Calderdale and Mid-Sussex all graffiti is painted over within 24 hours, in the belief that untreated it leads to more vandalism.

In Hartlepool it was noted that inappropriate structures were vandalised, but when replaced by the right kind of equipment, vandalism ceased (CASE-STUDY 5). In many case-study authorities, and certainly in the St George's Gardens case-study, park-users and professionals claimed that a rise in vandalism was associated with the loss of on-site parks staff, another argument for believing that in future site-based management and maintenance may help to restore public confidence in using parks and in reducing vandalism.

A sense of local ownership and pride can under some circumstances help to reduce vandalism. It is perhaps surprising how little graffiti is evident in the London Borough of Lambeth's parks. Even in areas where there are high levels of social disadvantage and the street fittings and shopfronts are often badly vandalised, the parks appear to remain unaffected. Lambeth's parks manager attributes this to the long-standing tradition of providing one o'clock clubs, after-school clubs, adventure playgrounds and summer playschemes in their parks - often in purpose-built buildings - which has meant considerable local attachment and affection for the parks and the facilities they offer to local communities (CASE-STUDY 24).

Dogs in parks

The presence of dogs in parks remains a contentious issue. To ban dogs from parks, even if it were possible, would at a stroke mean excluding one of the largest single groups of parks-users, the dog-owners themselves, who would claim to be among the most sociable, regular and vigilant groups of park-users. Yet dog fouling presents serious health hazards to young children, and can deter people from picnicking or playing games in parks. Some schools in several London boroughs have chosen not to organise games in parks any more because of dog fouling problems. In addition, many people find loose dogs very threatening, and will choose not to use parks because of the possibility of being harassed by a dog.

There are many schemes now operating in parks in Britain - dog toilet areas close to entrance gates, dog-free areas, poop-scoop schemes - yet none of them would claim to have completely solved the dog fouling problem. Interestingly in the Mid-Sussex case-study it appeared that bylaws were not the solution because of the difficulty of enforcing them, whereas in Calderdale bylaws enacted to require dog-owners to use poop-scoops in 12 named parks has been claimed a total success, because of the

widespread publicity surrounding the draconian fines (£500 for a single offence) and the council's publicised willingness to take people to court. Several authorities have supported events such as training days that encourage responsible dog ownership. Lambeth's Parks Services have recently launched a campaign on the need for people to control their dogs in parks and in other public places .

A question of priorities

It is unlikely in future that all public parks can - or should - be maintained to the same level. This is why strategies are important - to decide which functions each green open space should serve, and allocate resources accordingly. Yet each local authority will be aware of certain parks that have played a vital part in the social and public life of the community, and could continue to do so. In such parks high quality management and maintenance, acknowledging the park as a competitive leisure facility, is crucial.

This will cost money, of course, but so do other publicly provided leisure facilities, often with a much smaller cross-section of users. In the field of public leisure provision - sports centres, arts centres, public libraries, museums and galleries, nature conservation - parks have an equally strong case to argue in respect of their demographic reach and high levels of use - but this argument has yet to be clearly articulated and supported by evidence, as has begun in Cardiff (CASE-STUDY 20).

End of section checklist

- *Is there sufficient public consultation to support changes in maintenance regimes?*
- *Does the maintenance regime allow for the involvement of community groups and volunteers?*
- *Does the parks strategy take into account the needs of the elderly and people with disabilities?*

2.6 Building:

parks are also centres of activity

Parks and buildings go together

The idea that urban parks are essentially residual natural landscapes which should provide as little evidence of human presence or activity as possible, is an unhelpful myth that prevents them from playing a more vital role in contemporary life. The fact is that many of Britain's urban parks started off as the landscaped grounds of stately homes, or mansions of rich land-owning families and estates. For example, of parks mentioned in this report, Brockwell Park in Lambeth still has the Mansion House, as does Clissold Park in Hackney, Charlton Park in Greenwich and Shibden Park in Halifax. These parks were developed to provide a setting for large buildings, which in turn provided them with a focus and a function. That relationship between the 'grounds' and an active centre is now frequently forgotten.

Many Victorian parks were developed with additional visitor attractions, such as botanical gardens, and again the park was seen as the setting for uplifting or educational facilities. Trees, shrubs and flowers were labelled for edification; band-stands were built to promote Sunday concerts. An older tradition of urban pleasure gardens encouraged the idea that parks could be places of excitement and fun, providing music, fireworks, restaurants and drinking salons, dancing, theatre and masquerades. Only Battersea Park with its funfair site (a legacy from the Festival of Britain), zoo, athletics track, art gallery, pagoda, cafés and car parking for nearly 1,000 cars, and the Walsall Arboretum with its annual illuminations (CASE-STUDY 37) continue this tradition in any substantial way, although Shibden Park in Halifax appears to be developing in this direction.

Leisure centres and lidos

Buildings not only provide a focus, but can also provide some of the facilities needed for modern parks - toilets, refreshments, changing facilities - in a more managed and controlled way. This is why Mid-Sussex District Council has been keen to refurbish some of its parks by establishing at the heart of them leisure and child-care centres and other facilities, including cafés and refreshment kiosks. Newbold Comyn, an urban 'country park' in Leamington Spa, not only provides the site for the town's main indoor swimming pool and leisure centre, but also has developed a very successful barbecue area, where bays have been created with shrubbery for people to park cars and use the permanent barbecue stands for family picnics. This has proved enormously successful and families and works' parties plan weeks ahead for big gatherings with informal games and sports. In Lambeth's Brockwell Park, the Lido which had been closed for financial reasons for a number of years, was re-opened in 1994 by an independent company, Brockwell Lido, made up of ex-Lido staff, who run it with a grant from Lambeth Council, and have made a great success of it. Although the pool is shut for the winter, the café and restaurant remain open, as does South London's first Internet terminal base and therapy rooms. In the hot summer of 1995 the Lido was a magnet for tens of thousands of visitors, and the subject of a widely praised television documentary.

Cafés

Given a fairly high level of visitors, a café can provide a focal point for a park, and indeed some Corporation of London parks such as Highgate Woods and Golders Hill Park are noted for their friendly, usually family-run, cafés where people meet and sit talking for hours. The café in Hackney's Clissold Park is open every day, and on Christmas Day 1995 was busy from breakfast onwards. Successful catering franchises are difficult to establish, because of the seasonal and weekend nature of much park use, but where a local business can be encouraged to share some of the risks of running a park café, then the amenity, if not the financial, rewards to the park are often very high.

Calderdale's programme of parks self-management has focused on developing existing bowls clubs, and encouraging them to take on wider responsibilities. As the Wellholme Park in the Calderdale case-study shows, this has extended to the bowls club developing into a community centre, fund raising to provide a larger club house, providing a rota of volunteers to collect tennis court fees, pitch and putt fees, and establishing a well-used community facility in the centre of the park.

The importance of play provision

In Lambeth, at least thirteen parks offer building-based one o'clock clubs, open between 1pm and 4.30pm, four days a week throughout the year, open to anybody looking after children under five. In addition Lambeth Council provides 10 staffed adventure playgrounds and grant-aids another five, most of which are based in parks. These facilities provide a focal point and a 'heart' to many parks, which makes the park feel safer to other users because of the coming and going of carers with young children. Certainly in winter, it is reassuring to see lighted buildings in a park, filled with children and adults; much more so than if the park were just an empty, decorative landscape.

Children's play continues to be one of the primary reasons why people use parks. As the Stirling case-study (CASE-STUDY 11) shows, community consultation around local play needs, developing the whole of the park as a child-friendly environment (and not just one fenced-off corner of it), and working with children and parents to design and even make new play structures can be the key to the successful renewal of a neighbourhood park. Play structures, play equipment and purpose built children's toilets and first aid centre together make a regional attraction of Bath's Victoria Park, as another case-study shows (CASE-STUDY 13).

Other settings

In Bristol, Castle Park has been developed as a city centre amenity, with particular emphasis on a well-designed children's playground, but also as an outdoor gallery for a wide range of public art (CASE-STUDY 4). In Birmingham, Cannon Hill Park is the home of the Midlands Arts Centre, with a highly regarded programme of films, theatre and dance performances, art galleries, crafts workshops and other activities. The arts centre attracts children and their families (and school parties) who also get to know the park and may well re-visit on other occasions (CASE-STUDY 25). It also provides a café and bar that many park visitors use, and there is a strong cross-over of use between the centre and the park, although they are managed, staffed and serviced by two completely different organisations, the local authority for the park, and an independent charitable trust for the arts centre.

There can be problems with buildings in parks. Unused buildings, such as boarded-up administration blocks, cafés, toilet blocks, shelters or storage depots, can become a tempting target for arson and vandalism, as well as creating a sense of unease amongst park-users. Even buildings sited in parks in use, such as branch public libraries, youth centres, small museums, team changing rooms, can be become targets for vandalism at night.

However, in North America and in many European countries, parks are often naturally the home of museums, child-care facilities, art galleries, fairgrounds, and the answer to the problem of vandalism is not to empty the park even further of any kind of attraction or focal point, but to manage it more coherently as a local centre of leisure, recreation and social life.

End of section checklist

◆ *Has the authority explored with other service providers (eg health, education, childcare) the potential for joint developments in parks?*

◆ *Do the larger parks offer an appropriate infrastructure of toilets, refreshment services and other built amenities?*

◆ *Are play and facilities for children given a high enough priority in park management plans?*

Kite flying in Springfields Park, Hackney

Playgrounds attract children across a wide age range. West Ham Park (case-study 3.12)

Open-air Tai Chi classes, Clissold Park, Hackney

Photographs by Larraine Worpole unless credited otherwise

Brockwell Park Lido is run for the London Borough of Lambeth by an independent company formed by ex-council employees

Pensioners at a festival for the elderly in Clissold Park, Hackney

The bowls club at Victoria Park, Leamington Spa

Parks provide popular venues for outdoor entertainment. Here, the Wild Willy Barrett Band plays at the 1995 Campbell Park Festival, Milton Keynes (case-study 3.8) Photo: Anne Robinson

Ornamental gardens remain a popular feature of many parks, as here at West Ham Park (case-study 3.12)

Parks are a natural setting for informal socialising outside the home. West Ham Park (case-study 3.12)

The well-equipped
playground at Royal Victoria
Park, Bath attracts visitors
from a wide radius
(case-study 3.13)

A barbecue area has proved
a popular facility at
Newbold Comyn Park,
Leamington Spa

Parks are a feature of
everyday life for people of all
ages. St George's Gardens,
Camden (case-study 3.35)

Statues in parks provide visual - but sometimes vulnerable - links with local history.
St George's Gardens, Camden (case-study 3.35)

Sign at Royal Victoria Park, Bath states regulations in an informal way (case-study 3.13)

Clearly presented information for park users. Newbold Comyn Park, Leamington Spa.

An array of warning signs confront visitors to West Ham Park where regulations are rigorously enforced (case-study 3.12)

Sign of the times. Parks have a role in environmental strategies and as links in 'green' routes through urban areas

Fun and function: detail of a sculpted drinking fountain at Castle Park, Bristol (case-study 3.4) Photo: Sue Swingler

Popular activities such as boating help to attract visitors and provide a source of revenue and opportunities for franchising. Shibden Park, Halifax (case-study 3.19). Photo: Calderdale Council

Bringing the countryside to town: parks can give urban populations contact with the natural environment

Indoor activities at the King's Centre, East Grinstead, complement outdoor activities in the park around it

Open spaces with well-designed landscaping and planting can be as important in urban design as the buildings surrounding them. Centenary Square, Birmingham.
Photo: Neil Butler, Birmingham City Council

A café can provide a social focus for a park. The café run by an independent caterer in Clissold Park, Hackney, is open every day including Christmas Day when this photograph was taken.

*A 'Play in the Park' session at
Whins of Milton, Stirling
(case-study 3.11)
Photo: Sue Gutteridge*

*One o'clock club premises
provide social centres for
parents and children and help
promote local 'ownership'
and use of parks. Kennington
Park, London Borough of
Lambeth (case-study 3.24).
Photo: Sarah Wyld*

*People, parks and cities...
Parks provide a focus for the
communities they serve and
natural locations for
community activities and
celebrations*

2.7 Monitoring:

the 'how, why, when and where?' of park use

Demonstrating success

In his survey on the effect of CCT on parks, cited earlier, Bill Swan found that 65% of respondents (all park professionals) did not think that the parks in their authority met users' needs. This suggests that parks professionals either have an exceptionally pessimistic view of their achievements, or that they do not have the information on which to make proper judgements about the success or otherwise of the parks. In too many instances, the only measure of 'success' is to reach the end of the financial year without overspending the budget. Effective financial controls have to run in parallel with other targets, statements of purpose and procedures that help to make the service accountable to both staff and users. This section will illustrate questions of monitoring, the advantages of setting out aims and objectives and of promoting clear information to users.

Annual reports for parks

Although many authorities produce committee reports on parks for council members, very few produce annual reports designed to inform the park-users. The Milton Keynes Parks Trust does produce an annual report. The report is produced in a glossy A3 newspaper format: it reports on the year's activities; provides extracts from its annual accounts detailing the income and expenditure of the Trust; it publishes the results of the annual visitor survey, points out the comments people made and what the Park Trust has done and intends to do to address the concerns raised and it provides a list of events in the parks including attendance figures and mini-reviews. The report invites people to send in further ideas and explains the purpose of carrying out survey work. It contains feature articles on subjects such as wildlife and working as a volunteer with details of how people can find out more about volunteering opportunities with the Trust. The report gives

a summarised account of the landscape management tasks for the parks throughout the year, and gives names and contact numbers of Trust staff. Overall the annual report is a useful way of creating a clear identity for the parks service, promoting a sense of positive management of the parks, providing people with useful information and helping to establish contact between users, residents and the Trust staff.

The London Borough of Newham's draft Parks & Open Spaces strategy proposes the production of a simple annual report for the following reasons:

◆ To keep the Department's management focused on the achievement of results;

◆ To communicate information about the parks service to the public;

◆ To make a commitment to which a great many people both in and outside the council can contribute;

◆ To aid staff motivation by producing an opportunity to gain public acknowledgement for achievement.

The production of a simple annual report affords an opportunity for the parks service to summarise its achievements, to present its plans for the following year in a way that helps to create a distinct identity and invites public support and comment.

Parks charters

Charters for parks can be a useful way of promoting the service and setting out clearly and simply its objectives and what people can reasonably expect from their parks and how to make comments, suggestions or complaints. There is a danger that charters can too easily be bland statements of the obvious. On the other hand they can be useful tools in shaping a public profile of the parks service. The London Borough of Bromley found the process of writing a charter for the parks service and testing people's response to it a useful step in the process of developing their overall strategy for parks.

Similarly, Walsall Metropolitan Borough Council's Department of Leisure & Community Services found the process of applying for a Charter Mark a very useful one (CASE-STUDY 10). It describes the approach to setting standards and the 'Customer Service Contract' which covers standards of service, details of the cost of delivering the service, complaints procedures, details of market research and methods of monitoring. This contract is sent to all hirers of facilities of the arboretum including events organisers and sports clubs. The findings of surveys and questionnaires are published by way of press releases to local media. As part of the drive to improve relations between staff and users the Community Park Wardens receive 'customer care training' and take part in other such schemes developed nationally by the English Tourist Board. The charter application also outlines the complaints procedure, an approach to ensuring value for money and measurable improvements in the quality of service. The charter application highlights improvements in four main areas:

◆ Fabric of the park;

◆ Environmental issues;

◆ Services to customers;

◆ The arboretum as a venue for events.

The application also sets out the plans for the future. These include, the creation of an organic gardening centre, an expansion of the healthy eating initiative introduced by the catering DSO, the introduction of a walksafe scheme and an 'investors in people' programme.

The charter should endeavour to set targets, to provide overall coherence in the presentation of the service to the public and to set a standard for all staff involved in the parks.

Monitoring use

Lack of information about park use has been a hindrance to the development of parks as a vital urban amenity. Use of other leisure facilities can quite easily be monitored by turnstiles or computerised ticket sales. In the

case of parks it may seem an anathema to apply user research to what is widely regarded as a realm of freedom. However, park managers need to have good information about patterns of park use in order to make decisions about how best to develop the service.

Many local authorities now carry out basic monitoring exercises such as visitor counts and questionnaires and interviews with people in the parks. Simple monitoring exercises can be undertaken, including straightforward counts of all the people entering a park over a set period of time. Variations on this method include sampling numbers of users in one-hour time blocks at several times throughout the day. As well as simply counting, these exercises can record basic data such as whether parks visitors are:

◆ Male or female;

◆ Alone or in groups;

◆ Accompanied by a dog;

◆ Accompanied by children; and

◆ What time of day they are visiting.

These kinds of surveys are beginning to show common patterns of use such as the high numbers of park-users who walk to the park and that the majority of those interviewed live within a few minutes walk from the park. Perhaps the most important feature of this kind of survey is the picture it builds up over a period of several years. For example, a simple exit survey is carried out each year from the annual Illuminations event held in the Walsall Arboretum. The survey has now been carried for several years and it reveals useful information about changing patterns of use and changing attitudes. The results directly inform decisions about the programming, pricing, catering and management of the following year's event. Management decisions for Pallister Park in Middlesbrough are also informed by close monitoring of park use. Several surveys have confirmed the use of the park by elderly people and parents with young children which reverses previous trends. Where appropriate, such surveys should also be able to demonstrate park by park comparisons.

Household surveys

Household surveys provide a useful means of supplementing observation exercises and questionnaires carried out in parks. Unlike park-based surveys, household surveys include people who may not visit the park. Two small household surveys were undertaken as part of this study to provide supporting evidence of use for the case-studies. One was carried out in households around West Ham Park, the second around Poverest Park in the London Borough of Bromley. In each case 200 households were targeted. The results of these surveys show that 24% of the respondents said they had visited the park that day and 28% had visited within the last 7 days: these are high levels of frequency of use. Both surveys again provided confirmation of what are now fairly widely common patterns of park use, notably that: most people walk to parks; the most common reason given for using parks is to accompany children; that the age-range and social mixture is very wide; that most users claim to feel safe in their local park in daylight hours; and finally, that dog fouling remains the outstanding cause of complaint.

Only a small minority of people responding said they never used the park and of these several felt they were too old or had a disability that stopped them from using the park. The largest proportion of people who said they never used the park were those identified as over 60. The largest proportion of those who felt unsafe were again in the over 60 age group. These surveys showed that park managers need to consider ways to make parks more accessible to older people.

Market research

Once basic information about park use has been acquired, careful consideration should be given to the use of more sophisticated forms of market research. Ideally, research on park use should be able to make valid year by year comparisons and should be carefully directed to test the effectiveness of particular policies. However, market research can be a very expensive business and if undertaken has to be very carefully and precisely directed. The London Borough of Bromley carried out street interviews, household surveys and focus groups in order to research people's perceptions of the different kinds of parks in the borough. The research was carried out as part of the preparation of the strategy and was used to test the new categories of park types the borough was developing.

The Royal Parks Agency has commissioned a three year programme of survey work to collect information on the use of, and visitor attitudes towards, the Royal Parks. The objectives of the study are to discover and evaluate: the number and profile of visitors, the motivation for, and nature of, visits and the impression of satisfaction with the visit. It shows where park-users came from, how they travelled there, and whether they came alone or in groups. It provides some evidence of conflict between different uses (dogs, children, organised sports, traffic, cycling, ecology and contemplation) but suggests that such conflict is not widespread; and points to areas for improvement, especially facilities such as toilets, cafés, shelter and seating. The research provides an important base-line from which to continue to monitor changes in use and it enables managers to compare use between the parks.

Research raises the corporate profile

An important element of Watford Council's market research was based on a structured questionnaire completed by park-users. The research has proved to be very useful in establishing the improvements that park-users would like to see, but officers report that one of the main benefits of the research has been to prompt a debate ahead of the production of a council leisure strategy. The user research has raised the profile of the service and opportunities for development and these will now be incorporated into the leisure strategy. The officers felt that without such clear research evidence it would have been difficult to raise the profile of the parks service within the wider corporate strategy.

The prime considerations in monitoring park use should be to:

◆ Define the precise purpose of monitoring (to provide some initial figures, to test particular policies, to prepare for the introduction of specific changes in the park);

◆ Make sure that the same method can be used in successive years in order to allow for comparison over time;

◆ Ascertain use at different times of the year, (recent surveys in Watford show high levels of park use in winter);

◆ Make the exercise applicable to different parks and cross-park comparisons.

A combination of different techniques can provide a more rounded picture. Surveys undertaken outside the parks, either by street, telephone or household surveys will pick up views of people who, for whatever reason, do not use the parks.

Events are an important feature of the parks service and where possible records of numbers of people attending should be kept and used to inform decisions about future funding and support given to them.

End of section checklist

◆ *Does the local authority produce an annual parks report or other public information about parks services?*

◆ *Has the authority investigated developing park charters?*

◆ *What forms of market research are undertaken to inform parks policy?*

2.8 Involving:
working with communities

A wider portfolio

In the future local authorities may be responsible for a wider portfolio of open space, ranging from parks and allotments to newer initiatives such as community gardens and city farms. They will not necessarily run them all directly. Instead they will have a strategic overview as to how all these places complement each other, and they will facilitate community involvement and enable groups, clubs and individuals to get more out of a diverse mix of public open space. The involvement of various different community organisations in the facilities within local parks is a major theme for the future of public parks. This is not because 'community involvement' is a cheaper alternative to direct municipal management, nor is it the result of a sometimes over-simplified theory that 'local ownership' will reduce vandalism and its associated costs. Rather it is because partnerships with wildlife groups, sports clubs, one o' clock clubs and so on will release much more potential for parks to play a central role in urban life, a theme that is evident in many of the case-studies.

There is no one model for involving people in the organisation of events and activities within parks. Parks projects have taken place under the remit of creating 'safer cities', carrying out environmental education, 'urban forestry', arts projects, youth projects, and even health related activities. This section will draw particularly on three case-studies concerning community involvement posts - the Community Development post based in Bristol City Council's Parks service, the Metropolitan Borough of Walsall's Local Involvement Project and on the Safer Parks Co-ordinator based in Hartlepool Borough Council (CASE-STUDIES 2, 10 & 5). It will also consider other methods of achieving community involvement in the parks such as Friends groups, arrangements which encourage clubs and societies to manage parts of the park and the placing of community facilities such as one o'clock clubs in the parks.

Posts and programmes

The posts in Hartlepool and Walsall began as temporary projects. In Hartlepool the post of Safer Parks Co-ordinator was established as a one year temporary project financed by Teesside Training and Enterprise Council. Similarly in Walsall, the Local Involvement post began as a three year project to establish urban forestry, managed by the Black Country Urban Forestry Unit. The post was jointly funded by the Countryside Commission and Walsall Metropolitan Borough Council. Both demonstrate how temporary posts can help to precipitate more significant changes in approaches to park management. In Bristol, the post of Community Development Officer - Parks was established as a full-time post within Leisure Services. There are other examples of community development posts; the London Borough of Newham, for example, also has a full-time Community Projects Officer. Northamptonshire County Council have established a Pocket Parks Officer whose brief is to support community action in developing pocket parks. Other authorities such as Wrekin Council see community involvement not in terms of particular posts but as a core element of all the work undertaken by the Landscape Management Unit and other management units responsible for public parks.

Necessary skills

A background in environmental education and involvement in the voluntary sector is common to all three post-holders, and experience of community organisations such as city farms, the British Trust for Conservation Volunteers (BTCV) or community-based environmental regeneration schemes has influenced the way in which community involvement approaches have been developed in parks. To begin with, community involvement projects were seen as a means to an end - to create safer parks or to establish urban forestry; the greater benefits of generating real involvement by different local groups were discovered along the way.

In Bristol, the community development post was established as the result of the recognition that the role of the urban park was hard to define. Most parks are unstaffed; they are not as highly cultivated as they once were, and many contain 'wild' or ecologically managed areas. The division between formal and informal parks has been eroded by standardised maintenance procedures over recent years. The role of the community development worker was to re-connect park managers and park users.

This facilitating role is common to all the community involvement posts and projects. In Newham, the Community Parks Development Officer has established a network of local contacts and in so doing has paved the way for the introduction of the new Park Rangers Service whose role is dependent upon good links with a range of community organisations. In Walsall the concept of local involvement has influenced every area of park management, and made staff at all levels more open to the idea of community involvement.

Community involvement posts and projects work by creating a momentum or a focus for projects within and around the parks. Post-holders either support group activities or take on the responsibility of co-ordinating and arranging events. In so doing they provide a 'public face', a clear point of contact for people and groups who wish to take part in or run events. In Walsall and Bristol, the work of community involvement officers has been the key to establishing successful friends groups. In Hartlepool, the Safer Parks Co-ordinator operated as a catalyst, releasing the latent commitment from schools, old people's homes, local businesses, contractors and local clubs, to the improvement of the park.

Friends groups and other community organisations

As well as organising and facilitating events, the community involvement posts have been useful in creating a sense of openness on the part of councils to respond to the views and ideas of park-users. Friends groups or park action groups can set themselves up and operate entirely independently of community involvement posts. Nevertheless, these community posts help to facilitate constructive relationships between local groups and local authority parks management. In Bristol and Walsall, the officers have played an important role in establishing such groups.

The officers have been able to identify particular parks where local interest is strong, but has not been formalised. By calling a meeting, distributing newsletters and making links between different local groups they can help to establish viable park-based groups. They can provide advice to the friends groups, call meetings, provide basic resources such as maps and plans, bring in expertise such as landscape architects and facilitate connections between different community groups - as well as provide clear information about council practices and what the authority can deliver in terms of park management.

Park-based groups themselves can take very different forms. Some, such as wildlife groups, user groups, community gardeners or play groups are organised to further single objectives. Others, such as resident groups or friends groups may wish to have a greater general influence over park management decisions. The role of the community development worker is to support each group according to its own aims and objectives.

The setting up of park groups is a relatively new activity for local authority park managers. There is no single model. Some groups have formal constitutions. The London Borough of Wandsworth has established formal park consultative committees. Sheffield City Council has set up a city-wide Environmental Forum in order to bring together groups in the voluntary sector associated with environmental and parks concerns. The London Borough of Southwark is in the process of establishing an umbrella forum to bring together the five friends groups in the borough. In Camden, the Friends of St George's have even developed their own management plan for local debate.

Other authorities have been wary of friends groups, worried that they are unrepresentative. However, as long as all concerned are clear about the nature of the group, who it represents, what the broader policies of the local authority are, and where ultimate responsibility for decision-taking lies, then friends groups can have a beneficial effect on the park.

However, there are limits and pitfalls. The trust and commitment of friends groups can crumble when the council is seen to fall down on simple tasks such as basic repairs to pathways, replacing bins and benches. The credibility of the community development worker can be undermined if the glaring inability to sort out short-term repairs appears to make a mockery of even discussing longer term management ideals. A group that feels it has tried and been let down can be more embittered than if it had never tried at all.

The successful establishment of a local group or network can take time. Quite often the funding regimes of the authority don't allow for the slow pace of some groups to become established. Partnership bids have to be put together for a particular deadline, or some money becomes available for a children's play area and has to be spent within the financial year. Long-term strategies which allow for proper community involvement should help to overcome these difficulties. In some instances a simple leaflet drop to elicit interest in a tree-planting exercise can bring 100 people for one afternoon; in other areas generating interest and involvement in a local park will be a much more long-term project. Once established there is also a danger that a series of piecemeal projects can work against the overall unity of a park,

both in terms of management and in aesthetic terms. Therefore it is important that groups share the aims and objectives of a wider management plan for the park, and work within it, with guidance from landscape designers and park managers.

In summary, the success of the groups in Walsall and Bristol relied upon:

◆ Effort and commitment from a mix of local residents;

◆ Openness, honesty and optimism - the council officers should provide the parks groups with as much financial and other information as they need. A group cannot be viable in the longer term if it is based only on complaint;

◆ Avoiding smothering the group - in Walsall, friends group members described early meetings with the authority where the number of eager council officers present began to be overbearing. Direct contact with one of two key individuals from the authority proved to be more effective;

◆ Early successes can give the group a boost and raise its credibility within the local area;

◆ Good relations with other park-user groups;

◆ A good park to start with - a group is more likely to succeed when the park is central to an identifiable community, rather than part of a boundary between communities. If the park is already varied and interesting, the chances of establishing an effective group are greater.

Working with schools

Carrying out projects with schools has been one of the most important ways of establishing links between the parks service and the wider community. Environmental education is one of the core functions of the new parks ranger services which is now building on the pioneering projects of community involvement officers. The Safer Cities Co-ordinator in Hartlepool made contact with at least five different schools in the area around the park which formed the focus of her project, and the involvement of schoolchildren was a central feature to most of the subsequent events organised in the park.

A major element of work in Walsall undertaken by the Black Country Urban Forestry Unit (CASE-STUDY 17) were the school events designed to increase understanding of woodland ecology and the ecological value of trees. Parks staff came to realise that tree-planting, for example, provided a good way to make initial contact with schools and community groups and that these links can gradually develop into greater involvement in the parks. Independent agencies such as urban wildlife groups (CASE-STUDY 38), and projects such as the Centre of the Earth in Birmingham (CASE-STUDY 22) gained much of their momentum and public approval because of concerted programmes of work with schools.

Safer parks, safer cities

The link between safety and the recovery of parks for community use, is evident in the Hartlepool case-study, but elsewhere efforts are being made to 'crowd out crime' by making parks better used. The re-location of leisure facilities into parks in Mid-Sussex provides a stream of users and visitors as does the provision of one o'clock clubs in Lambeth's Parks. One of the key themes of the Pallister Park renewal programme in Middlesbrough was to reverse a pattern of neglect and vandalism by establishing a community centre in the heart of the park. The park, which is open from 10am to 10pm is supported by lighting and CCTV. Anti-crime measures such as the swift removal of graffiti, broken glass and other evidence of mis-use are strategies employed by a number of local authorities to assuage public perceptions of crime and vandalism. The London Borough of Sutton is experimenting with a new electronic system to speed up the process of monitoring vandalism and carrying out repairs to park property.

Consultation

Most authorities now see consultation with residents and local groups as a necessary

prerequisite to improving or making changes to a park. The purpose of consultation exercises varies from a simple check to test support for a proposed scheme to more open ended attempts to find out how a park might be developed in the longer term. Consultation is a key element of any post involved with community projects in parks. The community development worker in Bristol has developed some principles to help guide the process of consultation. Primarily, consultation implies a willingness to listen and to adapt ideas; if this is not the case, then the consultation exercise is about promotion or informing people of decisions that have already been taken.

Consultation can be complex, and therefore there needs to be clarity on the following points:

◆ Be clear about the purpose of consultation;

◆ Make explicit who will be responsible for making the final decision;

◆ Be clear about who is to be consulted;

◆ Tell people the results and inform them about any further stages.

Once these questions have been clearly established then there are a range of different methods that can be employed: from one-off meetings; letters to residents; notices in the parks; soliciting views from a range of existing organisations; door to door enquiries; formal or informal 'planning for real' exercises and longer term attempts to build agreement between people about the future direction the park should take.

Delegated management

Friends groups, community facilities and the management of park facilities by voluntary clubs, individual volunteers and societies all represent different forms and levels of community involvement. All can co-exist within the same park. In Willenhall Park in Walsall, for example, the Friends Group is involved in the decisions concerned with the overall management of the park and they co-operate with and support the Angling Club which has a 'stewardship arrangement' with the local authority to manage the fishing lake.

Walsall have also set up stewardship agreements with a number of bowling clubs in the town. The cost of maintaining greens is quite high and the fees for their use can be restrictive for some clubs. In return for a reduced fee, the club is expected to contribute to the management of the green usually by facilitating their wider public use (hiring out equipment and opening up public sessions) and by carrying out some improvements to the greens themselves. Other examples are provided in the earlier section on 'Managing'.

A role for volunteers

The involvement of volunteers in aspects of park development is an issue that needs careful consideration. Organisations such as city farms, Groundwork Trust projects and community gardens have a tradition of voluntary involvement. Public parks, on the other hand, are only beginning to consider the role of volunteers. Volunteering in parks can take many forms, including one-off conservation exercises, such as clearing streams and planting trees, organised and run by local wildlife or conservation groups which are voluntary organisations themselves. Events in parks such as the carnival in Rossmere Park in Hartlepool, depend upon voluntary effort from individuals and groups, to organise events, provide refreshments and so on.

The Local Involvement Project in Walsall has attracted volunteer input from students, who volunteer in return for assistance with dissertations and projects, and Morden Hall Park in Merton provides opportunities for a very small number of volunteers who wish to help in gardening and conservation work. However, such volunteers need close supervision and training, and should not be considered a form of cheap labour. Stewardship agreements and delegated management arrangements imply voluntary commitment from club members; other openings for voluntary involvement have to be carefully considered and monitored. The role of volunteers should be included and defined in a park management plan.

This emphasis on voluntary activity as part of the solution to urban environmental problems, echoes the call of the Rio Summit for urban sustainability (Agenda 21), to include more democratic forms of participation in local decision-making. Moreover, there is substantial potential for using parks issues to discover and involve new local constituencies in parks. This in turn can assist and enrich local authorities' own relationships with sections of their local populations.

> ### End of section checklist
> ◆ *Is there an understanding of the role parks can play in community development?*
> ◆ *Does the authority have the skills to work with community groups and Friends organisations?*
> ◆ *Is there a programme for working with schools?*

2.9 Funding:
partnerships and other funding programmes

In recent years parks services almost everywhere have lost funding, primarily as a result of:

◆ Budget cuts;

◆ Savings made as a result of CCT being diverted elsewhere;

◆ More powerful arguments for resources being made by other services within local leisure or environmental provision.

A starting point from which to argue for increased funding is the development of a coherent, manageable and credible strategy. This argument is dealt with at greater length in an earlier part of this report, and in several of the case-studies. It is also important to be convinced that there could and will be new sources of funding, whether in the form of direct financial inputs through lottery bids or single regeneration budget (SRB) bids, through partnership schemes, through the addition of new resources in kind, volunteer schemes and so on. In this section we briefly look at a number of such cases where new or levered funding has been made available to parks.

Civic renewal and civic pride

As the Ashford case-study demonstrates (CASE-STUDY 1), the decision to make the town the site of a new £80 million international passenger terminal for the Channel Tunnel link, created immediate pressures on the local authority to re-think the quality and amenity value of the town centre in which it was to be located, including the then sorry state of Victoria Park. The newly formed Landscape Development Team undertook a detailed survey of local attitudes towards the park, and plotted existing and possible new uses. The team rejected the idea of simply restoring a lost 'heritage' in favour of developing the park to meet modern needs and interests, and patterns of local life and leisure. Play facilities were central to the re-development of the park, as well as

developing a continuing events programme. Since 1992 more than £300,000 has been spent on the park, half of the money being raised from outside sources, largely as a result of having a clear 'masterplan' and 5 year financial projection of income and expenditure. The park was rejuvenated as part of a wider programme to restore the civic quality of the town centre to meet a new opportunity.

In Bury St Edmunds, Abbey Gardens in the town centre has been developed as one of the major tourist attractions in the city, and is a stopping off point for a considerable coach party trade. Based on a botanic garden created in 1821, the site remained in private hands until 1951 when it was bought by the borough council and developed even further with funding for the addition of a garden for the blind and rose garden. Abbey Gardens also has a playground, tennis courts, aviaries, a tea-room and a kiosk, and is serviced by two full-time resident park-keepers.

Urban regeneration

Quite different circumstances occasioned the refurbishment of the Barracks Park in Hulme, Manchester, and the proposal to develop a new park as a result of comprehensive re-development. In this case the wider programme was that of urban renewal, and completely re-fashioning of an area of Manchester that had become notorious for bad housing, high levels of crime, and severe demoralisation among many of the residents. These new resources resulting from a successful City Challenge bid are being managed by Hulme Regeneration Ltd, a joint venture company set up by Manchester City Council and developers AMEC involving the private sector. The starting point for making parks a central focus of the renewal strategy was an open space audit, which led to the agreement that any new park should not simply occupy space left over when all other uses were accommodated, but be part of a comprehensive re-linking of Hulme to its neighbouring areas, including the city centre, through the design of open space corridors and networks.

In many cases there is a general over-reliance on capital programme expenditure for the adaptation of public parks, largely as a result of the competing demands for revenue expenditure, which is not generally eligible for most forms of grant assistance. The very nature of capital programme expenditure also tends to favour infrequent, substantial intervention rather than the more modest scale, recurring expenditure needed to keep public parks fit for their purpose.

Private sector sponsorship

There has been a renewal of interest by the private sector in enhanced urban quality. For example, housing developers such as Pegasus Retirement Homes make a point of providing high quality open space in and around their projects. Brindley Place, part of Birmingham's new network of city centre spaces, is funded by a private developer. As the Castlefield case-study shows (CASE-STUDY 21), the private sector can become enthusiastic about and financially involved in partnership arrangements to fund and manage new urban spaces. In Ashford, local companies sponsored experimental play equipment. Sponsored events take place in parks, but direct sponsorship of parks themselves remains rare in Britain compared to North America, with its well known example of Central Park New York which is substantially funded by commercial sponsors.

Other partnerships

Throughout the country, local authorities are working with organisations such as the BTCV, Groundwork Trust and Common Ground as a way of bringing new resources into parks. As already noted, Southwark Council in partnership with Groundwork Southwark are involved in an ambitious programme to raise £30 million to regenerate Burgess Park as a local and regional amenity. The Quaking Houses case-study (CASE-STUDY 31) illustrates how Groundwork West Durham have been successful in raising finance from a

variety of sources to create a new community garden in a depressed mining village. In East Durham the Groundwork Trust is working closely with a number of local authorities on park regeneration strategies and programmes. As the Hartlepool case-study shows (CASE-STUDY 5), funding for the original 'Safer Parks' programme came through the local Training and Enterprise Council. In a number of local authorities BTCV are now seconding or under-writing the costs of a full-time volunteer officer to be based within the local authority structure to administer a conservation volunteer scheme.

Income generation

While the key feature and principle of public parks provision remains their free entry and access to all, this does not prevent the enhancement or development of support facilities and activities that can generate revenue, and park-users may be supportive of this if they can be re-assured that such revenue will be reinvested into the park to continue a programme of improvement. As the Shibden Park case-study shows (CASE-STUDY 19), this large landscaped park in Halifax is enormously popular with family, car-borne visitors in the summer months, and through a number of franchises - for cafés, refreshment kiosks, boating lake facilities, pitch and putt, and tractor train rides through the park - is able to generate income which is spent on promoting and maintaining the park as a regional attraction.

Many parks rent out space for seasonal circus or travelling fairground visits, or for sports events, festivals and other large scale entertainments. This can cause conflicts with residents living immediately adjacent or facing on to the park, who object to the noise and litter caused by crowds or live events; on the other hand, the park is a communal facility and ought to be a place of public celebration from time to time. If events are reasonably rationed over time, well managed and the park made good quickly following any large gathering, then the park can come into its own as a great gathering place and festival site for the whole community.

Battersea Park has a full-time events co-ordinator, providing an events programme throughout the year; in just one month, October 1995, this included sponsored walks, cycle racing, full moon celebrations by Buddhists at the Peace Pagoda, half marathons, custom car rallies and fireworks displays. Holland Park in Kensington is the home of an annual open air festival, with ballet, opera, classical and light music. Campbell Park in Milton Keynes is the site of an annual two-day world music festival, which includes performances by many local school drama groups, music groups, local writers' workshops and religious choirs. The site was developed with water and electricity supplies laid permanently to the festival arena in act of forethought. Many of these festivals are funded from other departmental budgets, or with grants from regional arts boards and private sponsorship, and thus effectively bring additional resources to the park, making it a livelier and more intensively used place. In Leamington Spa's historic town centre park, Jephson Gardens, some floral displays are sponsored by local companies.

Greenwich Council has made a great success of generating revenue from film and television companies encouraged to use Greenwich parks as locations for filming. The council has a full time Sponsorship Co-ordinator within the Leisure Services Marketing Unit, and in 1994 worker raised £70,000 in filming fees throughout Greenwich. Location filming also spawns invisible income in the spin-off activities of catering, parking and other services. Charlton House in Charlton Park was used by the BBC for 'A Question of Attribution', by LWT for an Agatha Christie 'Poirot' episode, and for the film 'Porterhouse Blue'. Maryon Wilson Park in Greenwich was the eerie setting for the film 'Blow-Up', now part of local mythology. Of the revenue generated, the Marketing Unit keeps a percentage and the rest is returned to the appropriate departmental budget. At present many parks are used occasionally for TV and film location shooting, but few if any local authorities have fully developed policies (and charge rates) to cater to this growing industry; as a result many forego valuable income, since they charge on a haphazard basis, or in some cases fail to charge at all.

Lottery funding, particularly from the National Heritage Memorial Fund (NHMF), is also likely to be a source of funding for urban parks renewal and development schemes, indeed urban parks have been named as a one of the priority areas for funding. The Heritage Lottery Fund has produced a set of guidelines for applicants for their 'Urban Parks Programme', in which they state that:

> *'With lottery money, we want to encourage new ideas and to galvanise thinking about how such places (urban parks) can play a more fulfilling role in the life of the community around them.In order to give special encouragement to applications in this field, we will be giving priority to the theme of urban parks for at least the next three years.'*
> *NHMF January 1996*

In short, there are a number of sources of finance and other forms of support available to local authority parks services, given a clear strategy to guide the fund-raising and partnership programme, though these are likely only to amount to a small proportion of the mainstream budget needed to maintain basic quality standards in green space management and maintenance across any one borough.

End of section checklist

◆ *What role do parks play in urban regeneration and economic development programmes?*

◆ *Does the parks department have a fund-raising strategy?*

2.10 Moving on:

parks help create better cities

A better quality of life

Urban parks are an enormous resource for towns and cities and there are opportunities for them to contribute much more to improving the quality of urban life. Developing parks includes making the most of events in the parks, it means making parks work to meet the corporate objectives of the authority in terms of regeneration, education, improving health and making a contribution to urban sustainability. Parks are ripe for the introduction of many new skills, in programming, children's play, arts projects, community development, franchise management, ecology, sports, health and fitness, landscape design and many others. Over the last four years, the contracting out of park maintenance has pre-occupied many dozens of authorities; now that most contracts are in place, authorities are beginning to turn to questions of how best to develop their parks service.

Programming

The programming of parks is an essential part of their management. Events from large festivals to school sports days help to tie the park into the life of the neighbourhood. The greater the number and diversity of events in parks, the more people are likely to be involved in some way or other in them. Whilst the large festivals can help to promote the borough and gain good publicity for parks, smaller scale events regularly held are just as important in helping to create a sense that the park is a safe, well-used facility, that is being positively managed.

Successful parks programmes include a very wide range of different activities many of which only involve small groups of people. The dawn bird walks led by parks staff in Hounslow for example, may attract only a handful of people, while Asian melas, Gay Pride festivals and radio roadshows can attract national audiences.

Certain parks are particularly suitable for staging a large number of events. The International Balloon Fiesta at Ashton Court Estate, Bristol, is the biggest free spectator event in any public park in the UK, attracting over half a million people. The Arboretum in Walsall still stages its annual illuminations supported by six weeks of programmed events which attract 300,000 visitors every year, while Battersea Park stages events in the park all year round and attracts an estimated three million visitors a year. Battersea Park has an events team based in the park. They are geared to manage every detail and can provide an events operator with a complete package covering security, parking, tents, toilets and so on. Battersea Park now raises significant income from events. Parks can be very significant players as venues for major urban events.

In complete contrast, small scale activities (fetes, bulb planting days) became the backbone of the safer parks programme in Rossmere Park in Hartlepool. It was through the small scale activities that local schools, old people's homes and local businesses had the opportunity to become involved in the park. Similarly, events such as 'park walks' held as part of the Black Country Urban Forest Unit's projects, brought to light people's memories and details of the history of the parks involved.

Cannon Hill Park in Birmingham has a programme of children's events in the park and together with the West Midlands Arts Centre the park runs a series of summer children's activities. The park now supports a number of attractions for children - the Nature Centre, the children's playground and the facilities at West Midlands Arts Centre (including its classes for children) - and these have given the park a good reputation as a place for people with children to visit. The arts centre bar and café have become popular with families especially at weekends, as (unlike many pubs and restaurants) it provides one of the few places where families can socialise together.

Parks are also used informally as places for social events - children's parties, picnics, religious celebrations and weddings. Morden Hall Park in Merton, South London is the location for the Borough Registry Office and because of its position in the park is a very popular wedding venue which is now attracting custom from outside the borough. The Pumphouse in Battersea Park is now licensed to hold weddings. The popularity of parks as a backdrop for wedding photographs indicates the potential for parks to cater for such needs.

Parks police

Nearly all park surveys show that visitors would feel safer if the parks were staffed. The loss of the park-keeper has created a problem of how best to maintain visible staffing. It has also opened up opportunities for developing new kinds of staffing roles in parks. The balance currently being played out in the introduction of new staff in parks is between a security role or a more interpretative service centred model of a ranger service. Many authorities are introducing a combination of both.

The London Borough of Wandsworth has been operating a Parks Constabulary Service for the past five years. They provide cover for all the borough's parks and open spaces under the Greater London Parks and Open Spaces Act 1967, which allows for staff to be sworn in as constables for the purpose of enforcing the bylaws. Officers of any newly formed constabulary service need to be properly trained. They must be fully aware of the Codes of Practice of the Police and Criminal Evidence Act (1984), and require training in first aid, self-defence and training in how to deal with every aspect of the management of public disorder. The powers of a Parks Constabulary include: power of arrest; seizure of dangerous dogs and the issuing of verbal and written warnings to offenders.

Parks police services are adopted in order to present a positive approach to tackling vandalism and damage to public parks; to reassure the public with a security presence and either to strengthen the powers of staff or to release ranger staff from law and order concerns in order to concentrate on parks development issues. The Wandsworth Parks Constabulary regularly make arrests and carry out successful prosecutions for offences against the bylaws. However, other boroughs have experienced some problems of confrontation between parks police and local youths, and the Metropolitan Police are said to have expressed some concern over the growth of private parks police services. The establishment of a parks constabulary is an expensive operation and there are serious pitfalls if attempts are made to set up forces without full and comprehensive training and management.

Parks rangers

Other authorities have been developing the ranger service to perform a more interpretative service development role. Birmingham's parks rangers now help to run events in the town centre; Walsall's park wardens have been redesignated Community Park Wardens and have a brief to perform more of a community development role. Southwark Parks Service has been developing a new ranger service over the last two years. The borough began with a small team of highly qualified rangers with backgrounds in environmental education and have developed competencies, defined skills and training needs necessary to bring the existing parks-based staff into the ranger service and to develop a more active parks staff competent to run events and work with schools and a range of other community groups. The Southwark model is based on a multi-disciplinary approach bringing together community development, arts, sports and leisure activities with environmental and educational approaches (CASE-STUDY 34). In its commitment to developing NVQ standards for ranger services, Southwark have begun to address the outstanding issue of the educational needs for managers of urban parks.

The development of the ranger service in this way makes the service more open to a range of other new skills. Southwark have been building up information and interest about health issues and park use. As well as measures associated with exercise, walking, and children's health, the rangers service has been working with health agencies to provide health information to drug-users. Similarly, Hounslow's Parks Services Officers support the borough's corporate HIV/AIDS policies by providing information about AIDS Helpline telephone numbers. Birmingham Leisure Service's Fitness Development Officer has begun to develop links with the parks staff and particularly park rangers to further a 'walking for healthy living' programme. She is keen to establish marked out walking routes in the parks for use by people on 'exercise on prescription' schemes (CASE-STUDY 32). In Stockport work is underway on a series of local maps describing 10 minute, 20 minute and longer walks which can be made from any district, as part of a joint health promotion, many of which are based in parks (CASE-STUDY 36).

Parks-based projects

A number of other parks-based projects indicates the potential to introduce new skills into the parks service. The community development workers in Bristol and Newham have been very important in paving the way for the introduction of ranger services. The skills involved in facilitating meetings, setting up friends groups, in resolving conflicts in parks are easily under-estimated.

Lambeth regularly draw on leisure centre recreation staff to run and manage outdoor sporting events in parks. The London Borough of Merton employed an artist to run a series of projects with schools and youth clubs in partnership with Wimbledon School of Art. This led to a number of very successful arts projects in parks (and in school grounds). The arts projects which usually lasted several weeks provided a point of interest and activity in the park (CASE-STUDY 26).

Parks-based projects such as those carried out by the National Urban Forestry Unit, the Groundwork Trust, Wandsworth's Ecology Officer and Hounslow's Green Strategy have introduced many different facets of ecology and ecological management skills into the parks. Bromley's park strategy has introduced multi-disciplinary teams which mix the skills of wardening staff, horticultural, rangers, events staff, ecological and landscape skills. Instead of being brought in to complete one-off schemes, the landscape officers have continued to become fully involved in the development of the parks service as key members of the multi-disciplinary parks team. The teams allow for a wide range of different professional perspectives and team members can develop their professional perspective within a wider framework of shared objectives. As the Centre of the Earth in Birmingham shows, environmental education can be a powerful draw for local young people.

Various park-based projects (Safer Parks, Hartlepool; Local Involvement, Walsall) have involved people with previous experience in the voluntary sector. They have brought with them new skills of marketing, desk top publishing for simple promotional material, public relations and good media experience, encouraging community action, volunteering and introducing some of the skills of fund-raising.

Parks and city centre regeneration

Past research has described the way in which local authority parks departments had become marginalised within local authorities and detached from mainstream corporate concerns. Parks managers need to re-connect the service to the core corporate policies and raise the status of the service. Town centre regeneration has been one area where parks have begun to be valued for the contribution they can make as part of a network of public spaces in town centres. Birmingham does not have a major town centre park but has included small parks and churchyards within the streets and squares strategy mixing green space, with squares, canalside walk ways and other pedestrian areas. The small parks help to support the mix of uses in the city centre as they serve both the residential, working, shopping and tourist visitors in the city.

Castlefield Urban Heritage Park in Manchester is an innovative development that does not fit into familiar definitions of a public park, rather it is one of the few true innovations that has underlined the regeneration of the Castlefield area of the city centre (CASE-STUDY 21). Although it is a mix of different aspects of industrial heritage and mainly an area of 'hard landscaping' virtually all its open spaces are accessible to the public and are mainly dedicated to leisure activities. The Castlefield Management Company run a visitor centre and a ranger service and help to run and promote events in the area. West Park in Wolverhampton is seen as a major potential benefit to the town centre, which means the park is taken into account in the debate about the town centre strategy and in new approaches to transport, economic development, tourism and so on. Albert Park in Middlesbrough town centre is also subject to a re-thinking of the role of a town park in a modern city centre. The council and the university have been exploring the potential for partnership to make more of Middlesbrough's town park.

Parks and housing

New parks can also play an important role within new housing areas. The new park planned as part of the regeneration of Hulme in Manchester is at the centre of the emerging plan for the public realm (CASE-STUDY 7). In Hulme it is hoped that the public park will be a symbol of environmental quality by which the area will become known and valued. The consensus between the community and all those involved for creating a park was not a plea for 'more green space', as Hulme, like many other housing estates, had ample green space - but it was so run down and meaningless that it had a detrimental effect overall. Despite deficiencies in the green space they were familiar with, the community still believed in the viability of a park. Through a sustained consultation programme a plan for a modern park is

emerging. What is clear is that, unlike far too many housing developments, the park will not simply occupy an area of left over land but will be carefully sited in the light of extensive consultation, an open space audit and a study of the local public realm of streets, squares, cycleways and green spaces. The 'towers in the park' concept was typical of the 1960s approach of building tower blocks and maisonettes set within anonymous open space. As these estates come around for re-furbishment the question of how to approach the open space can get lost between the numerous agencies involved. The Nechells Development Framework and the Bordesley Village Framework in Birmingham included strategic green plans which proposed the development of neighbourhood parks to be fully integrated within the housing areas.

Within the building industry various schemes are in operation to encourage good practice in regard to supporting the natural environment, such as the Green Leaf Housing Awards presented by the New Homes Marketing Board. However, much more can be achieved by housing developers, particularly housing associations, in the creation of innovative areas around new housing.

Parks and health

The connection between the management and use of parks and open space and new approaches to questions of public health policies are emerging. Although GP referral schemes mostly operate within leisure centres, there is some evidence that 'exercise on prescription' can be extended and applied outdoors. Increasing healthy activity in everyday life is an area of health promotion that is beginning to be developed and is very suitable for promotion in parks. The London Borough of Southwark held a conference in 1994 which began to explore areas of joint work between public health workers and parks managers.

Horticultural therapy is emerging particularly in the botanic gardens, but also in public parks. Battersea Park for example, has a small horticultural therapy garden. The psychological benefits of working with plants is currently being developed in a number of projects; typical of these is the Hilltops Nursery Project based in a hospital grounds in south London. The nursery, set up in 1991 under the auspices of the local health authority, is used by people suffering from mental illness. Recently, the nursery has been able to sell the plants and shrubs it has grown to raise income. The nursery has been exploring the possibility of expanding to public park sites and using redundant greenhouses.

The Metropolitan Borough of Sandwell and Tipton City Challenge have made health a focus for the Tipton regeneration strategy. Their proposal brings together primary health care and education facilities in a new 'Health Park' within the town centre. The intention is to set the healthcare facilities within an attractive park surround that reflects themes associated with health, fitness and relaxation.

Parks, sustainable development and Local Agenda 21

Agenda 21 is the name given to the programme of action for achieving the more sustainable forms of development agreed at the 1992 'Earth Summit' in Rio de Janeiro. It is one element in a larger debate about 'sustainable development' which is generally understood to mean an approach to development that combines economic, social and environmental concerns and is less wasteful and more efficient in the use of natural and material resources. The perspective is an important one for the future of cities, and park managers can explore ways of making parks part of a debate about sustainability. The London Borough of Sutton has initiated a comprehensive approach to the development of Local Agenda 21, much of which is applicable to the borough's parks. The community partnerships initiative includes friends groups, tenants groups, an allotments strategy and so on. Many parks have set up low level re-cycling schemes such as collection points for Christmas trees and garden waste, but there is clearly much more potential for parks to play a fuller role in the re-cycling and management of waste.

The 90 or so different urban wildlife groups around the country have led the way in all sorts of different nature reserves, many of which are in parks and are carried out in partnership with local authorities. The Wildlife Trusts have also collaborated with other environmental groups to develop sustainability indicators.

In the following case-studies, evidence is provided as to exactly how, why, when and where, new initiatives are being made; initiatives which put the importance of urban green space back into the mix of urban vitality, sustainability and quality of life.

End of section checklist

◆ Does the authority have an events programme for parks?

◆ What staffing arrangements are being used to ensure safety and community contact?

◆ Is the parks service exporting greening strategies to the rest of the Borough in partnership with housing, transport and planning services?

◆ Is the parks department fully integrated into local strategies for Agenda 21?

3.1 Civic renewal:

Victoria Park, Ashford, Kent

Key themes
- Individual park management plan
- Multi-disciplinary team
- Partnership funding
- Children's play

The redevelopment of a park

Victoria Park is the main town centre park in Ashford. As with many other urban parks, it had declined during the 1980s. To make matters worse, it was badly damaged by the storms of 1987 and 1990, and half the trees were destroyed. The park became an area of bare grass and crumbling asphalt paths with a basic play area, although it still had its main original feature, the Hubert Fountain, donated to Ashford in 1912.

On the other hand, Ashford itself was facing a new era of development as it became the site of a new £80 million international passenger station for the Channel Tunnel link -"the last stop before the tunnel" - or the first stop in Britain. The siting of the new station increased the pressure for growth and people began to turn their attention to the sorry state of the park. Victoria Park is an important walk through, connecting people with the town centre, lying only 10 minutes walk away from the new passenger station.

Preparing the ground

The borough council re-organised their staff structures in the early 1990s. The first job of the new Landscape and Conservation Team was to look at Victoria Park. They began by carrying out detailed survey work. The results highlighted the importance people attached to:

- Play areas;
- Woodland areas;
- The park as a meeting place.

The team began to carry out a series of analytical exercises; they set out to understand the park from every angle.

They:

- Plotted people's use of the park;
- Carried out interviews with people both inside and outside the park;
- Carried out a topographical survey;
- Examined its ecological state, including its water courses;
- Analysed its spatial attributes;
- Carried out an arboricultural survey;
- Looked at issues to do with access to the park, both by foot and by car;
- Looked at circulation within the park and the 'desire' lines where people had left the tarmac paths and carved out their own muddy tracks in order to take more direct routes;
- Recorded the local history of the park .

The masterplan

The results, analysis and synthesis of the survey work was reviewed by a working group of councillors and officers, and eventually a plan was produced for the revival of the park. The historical analysis showed that Victoria Park was never considered to be a fine example of a Victorian park, and so the pressure to 'restore' the park to a 'former glory' was reduced and this gave the team an opportunity to consider its modern role as a leisure resource. The park proposal poses the question:

How are local authorities to re-shape their parks in an age which constantly has to redress issues about social relationships and personal responsibility, an age which values individuality and is so uncertain about defining a coherent code of community behaviour?

The work programme

The first issue to be tackled was the storm damage. With a grant from the Countryside Commission, work was carried out on replacing lost and damaged trees and restoring the structure of the park with avenues of oak, chestnut and plane. The Ashford Conservation Volunteers did a simple leaflet drop around the neighbouring housing which brought out 50 people who helped re-plant trees.

Playgrounds

The second issue was the children's playground. After consulting a research team from Leeds Metropolitan University the team decided to build their own equipment. With earthmounding, landscaping and the use of specially built equipment they tried to create as many imaginative games as possible within the play area. Seating was included within it, rather than around it, and there are sheltered areas where children can play unseen. There are experimental pieces, including sound tubes that run underground which can be used by children to speak to each other. This play area is totally surrounded by a moat which serves to keep dogs out. Children can either scramble over or cross by one of the footbridges into the play area. Using moats means that the sight lines are clear and the playground is more obviously part of the wider park.

The playground was completed in 1992 and has proved very popular. A second playground designed for older children has also been installed. It is based on an assault course with climbing walls and an aerial cableway. This area also includes some innovative features such as two satellite dishes set 70 metres apart, aligned so that people standing at each one can communicate as the sound is transmitted acoustically from one to the other. The dishes were sponsored by a local cosmetics company.

Cycle track

The main avenue through the park is also a competition standard cycling track. The avenue is a wide aesthetically pleasing walkway that can be easily adapted into a competition cycling circuit. It was partly funded by a grant from the Sports Council. The park is well used for cycling events

which bring in people and provide an evening use for the park. The cycle track is 1.2 kilometres long and is regularly used for evening training sessions and for special cycling events. The Sports Development Team run weekly evening race programmes for different age groups; two weekend races are held each month as well as a number of cycling events organised by cycling clubs. Local schools and police hold cycling proficiency events on the circuit, which is also used by local road running groups.

The importance of design

The re-design of the park has highlighted some key design principles considered by the landscape team to be of great importance to the long-term success of the park. These are based on a view of design as an integral part of every aspect of park development, including consultation, management and long-term adjustment and maintenance.

To be properly informed the design team should never start with a blank sheet. The team argue that good design in the public realm must be comprehensively informed by the needs of users, and that function rather than aesthetics is paramount.

The team must be good at interpreting people's comments and their use of places. The interpretation of use has to inform the selection of materials used in the park's redevelopment. In Victoria Park, rather than using off-the-shelf pedestrian barriers, railings were made to designs based on the park's river.

The design team considered ways of finding multi-uses for areas of the park. The main 'carriage way' through the park also doubles up as a cycling track. Part of the main path can also be used as a small hard surface basket ball area. Where possible the design team used surplus Council materials, such as tree stock and rocks. The design of Victoria Park also took account of the need to create interest all year-round.

The design of the park also took account of its strategic position within the town. The park has been incorporated into the 'green

corridor' with cycling and walking tracks, supported by proper signage, that leads into the town centre past the International Station.

The design team needs to adopt the site. The design of a park is never complete. Modifications will be necessary as patterns of use become evident. The team needs to monitor use and keep in contact with users and should therefore be committed to maintenance.

Finance

The careful planning for the improvements to the park means that the authority has managed to attract outside grants. The Borough Treasurer agreed to match income gained externally pound for pound for capital expenditure. The first year the improvement programme was boosted by a grant from Task Force Trees, the sum was matched by the council; the second year a grant from Kent County Council was again matched by the council and the third year the Borough matched a grant from the Sports Council. The borough has spent £300,000 on the park since 1992; half the money came from outside grants and a small amount from corporate sponsorship.

The playgrounds incorporated many pieces of specially built play equipment; these turned out to be cheaper than buying standard pieces of play equipment. The team also incorporated old gas pipes and tyres donated by local companies. By building their own playground, they estimate they made savings of around £40,000.

The maintenance contracts have been upgraded to cope with the new design of the park. They include better inspection of play equipment and higher standards of maintenance in some areas while others have been left with less intense maintenance. Areas of grassland have been left to grow, hedge cutting has been reduced and riverbank flailing has been reduced. This has allowed for more time and money to be spent on the play areas and the formal areas of the park. Some areas of the park now cost marginally less to maintain than before.

Public appreciation

Surveys, consultation and visible re-development of the park have led people to make further constructive criticism.

'I was very impressed by the adventure playground in Victoria Park especially as there is a climbing wall. My partner and I enjoy rock climbing as a hobby, but we have to travel quite a long way to practice our hobby or to train at indoor climbing centres, so we were delighted to find that we can train in our home town. Although I realise it is intended as a children's playground, us adults also get a great deal of enjoyment out of it too! I just wanted to write to you and let you know that this is the best new development in the town for years.'

◆ ◆ ◆

'A very good idea, installing picnic benches and tables in Victoria Park. May I also suggest a coin-operated ladies convenience, or an attendant to be on hand, so that the public can use the loo. The door is always locked, and no one in sight to open it'.

The redevelopment of Victoria Park highlights some key themes:

◆ A commitment to regenerating the park in line with the modern leisure needs of the town as a whole rather than attempting a restoration of the park. Thus, the park contains two play areas, an events terrace, lighting, and a new sports area. It is a venue for festivals and other outdoor events.

◆ The changes made to the park were based on a series of in-depth surveys which were analysed and used to inform a development plan.

◆ The masterplan provided a clear base from which to apply and win external funds.

◆ Links with the local voluntary and business sector released voluntary labour, donations of material, loans of equipment and small scale sponsorship.

◆ The Landscape Team were prepared to build and commission original pieces of play equipment, which they believed, after carrying out research, would be more interesting for children.

◆ The inclusion of a high quality cycle track has been a useful way of making greater use of the park, particularly in the evenings. It has also provided the park with a unique additional facility which, when not in use, is an attractive pedestrian route.

◆ The re-design of the park has led to a new maintenance contract which provides for a much more effective use of resources. The revenue costs incurred by the maintenance of new facilities in the park have been reduced or partly offset by making savings elsewhere.

Contact: Mark Carty,
Deputy Leisure Services Officer,
Ashford Borough Council, Civic Centre,
Tannery Lane, Ashford, Kent TN23 1PL
Tel: 01233 637311

3.2 Community development in Bristol's parks

Key themes
- New skills
- Community involvement
- Consultation
- Events

Community involvement is generally thought to be an important feature of successful park management. However, there is little evidence available to show how this can be done. Bristol City Council has employed a community development officer, Michele Wood, within the parks service for the past six years.

Bristol Community Development Officer - Parks

The post was set up in 1989 following a re-organisation of the then Parks Department in preparation for CCT. The main purpose of the job is to: encourage, promote and assist with community development schemes in the community parks.

Community development in parks?

Community involvement ties in with a role for local government as an enabler, devolving, delegating and creating consensus. It is in part a recognition that local government can no longer take exclusive responsibility for the management of public facilities such as public parks.

Public parks have changed; the role of urban open space is not as easy to define as it once was. Part of Bristol City Council's response to these changes was to employ a community development worker to clarify needs and opportunities for urban parks and to provide a link between park managers and park-users.

A community development approach to parks is very useful in dealing with the complexities of providing for a wide range of people with differing expectations. The management of public space must acknowledge the sometimes difficult

conflicts that arise between people over its use. Often, simple questionnaires cannot deal with the underlying complexities and potential areas of conflict. The community development approach allows for an in-depth exploration of people's concerns and aspirations for parks.

Community development projects

Community development works by building on the interests and concerns of the existing local networks, of voluntary groups, residents associations, schools and many others. The worker helps to organise various events in parks such as tree planting, making ponds, carrying out nature and wildlife conservation.

The Parks Community Development Officer helps to set up park-based groups, provides support to existing groups and helps to conduct consultation exercises. In this work the officer can draw on expertise within the authority such as landscape architects, conservation staff, park rangers and a number of other voluntary organisations in the city.

Park-based groups can take different forms. Some, such as groups primarily concerned with wildlife or in setting up play facilities, are organised to further single objectives. Others, such as residents' groups or friends' groups may wish to have greater general influence over park management decisions. The role of the community development worker is to support each group according to its own aims and objectives.

Supporting community groups

The process of setting up a group may be slow. It can take about a year for the group to become established. During this time the group will need to achieve something practical and work out its organisation. It has to find ways of dealing with disagreement and ways of respecting every group member's point of view.

Firstly, groups are more likely to succeed:

◆ If the park is central to an identifiable community, rather than part of a boundary between communities, and if it is small enough to have a clear local identity (up to 50 acres), rather than being a park for the whole city.

◆ If the park itself is varied and has clear potential to appeal to different interests (e.g. wildlife, children's play).

◆ If the park is overlooked by housing and used as a short cut so that people already have close daily contact with it.

Secondly, there are issues that relate to the group themselves:

◆ The group needs to have enough people. It can be helpful if people did not previously know each other as pre-existing sub-groups can make it more difficult for new people to join.

◆ The group must be positive, enthusiastic and optimistic. Although groups often do start in opposition, perhaps, to threatened land, they need something

more positive to keep together after the resolution of the immediate threat.

◆ Members should see themselves as reasonably equal. Everyone should feel welcome and able to contribute. The group should also be able to deal with debate and conflict.

◆ People need to be in a reasonably settled position in their lives to make a commitment (even short-term) to joining a group.

The formal status of park-based groups can vary from informal temporary action groups to formally constituted consultative panels. There is a temptation for local authorities to encourage the establishment of model groups with identical constitutions and roles. This should be resisted.

Groups putting in grant bids often have to produce a constitution. When this is necessary the development worker tries not to use off-the shelf copies but helps the group to produce a constitution that suits their particular needs. It will describe the aims and objectives and how the group is organised. Most groups do require some named officers, particularly a treasurer.

The long-term low level support that groups receive from the community development worker and other council officers, including park rangers, landscape managers and landscape architects is important to the success of park groups. Once a group is formed and established it can operate largely independently of the council, but it still needs some support and liaison if organisation is not to become a burden to those involved. In Bristol, Michele Wood provides support to such groups.

Consultation

It is notoriously difficult to carry out successful and meaningful consultation with people about the management and maintenance of public parks. Consultation is an important part of the officer's work and over the years she has established some basic principles to guide consultation exercises. These are:

Be clear about why you are going to consult

Why is consultation necessary? Is the object of the exercise about how to spend additional money or is it about making financial savings? Is the aim to gather new ideas and local knowledge? Does the subject of the consultation exercise appear to be clear cut or complicated? Are the potential participants open-minded or are there already entrenched and have fixed positions? What is at stake?

Who will be responsible for making the final decision?

People who are being asked to take part in a consultation exercise need to know who will make the final decision. Will it be a known group of users or residents? Will it be the officers involved in the consultation? Will it be a council committee or even a more distant agency of government?

Who is to be consulted?

Is the consultation to be based on a local area, if so, how will it be defined? Which interest groups should be consulted? Which risk being left out? If the consultation is small-scale, the aim should be to reach everyone. If it is larger in scale then it will have to be based on some kind of model of representation.

Tell people the result

People should be told of the result of the consultation and what will happen next.

The skills of the community development worker

Parks are expected to cater for a range of diverse needs. Building consensus is seen as a way forward and is part of the skill of community development.

Some meetings stand out in my recollection as the moment when dissimilar people have accepted each other's membership of the group. I remember one meeting when people with diametrically opposed ideas were able to discuss an issue very calmly in a charged atmosphere and find a solution that was more creative than either of the original ideas. I am glad that the City Council can be involved with residents at a deeper level than public meetings and consultative papers. I have hugely enjoyed discovering other people's ideas and theories about what helps and what hinders people working together and have felt privileged to be part of so many groups.
COMMUNITY DEVELOPMENT WORKER -PARKS

Clearly, the Community Development Worker has to be skilled in running and facilitating meetings that help to find creative solutions to problems of management and conflicting views about appropriate development of parks.

Summary

◆ There is no single model for community development in parks. However, it does require good local knowledge, ability to facilitate public meetings, to administer and support groups, to identify opportunities for development, and to carry out effective and fair public consultation.

◆ Groups can take different forms. The officer has to support each group to help it achieve its own aims, whether they be in support of new play areas, wildlife habitats or the concerns of residents or tenants groups. The community development officer should play a significant role in consultation exercises, often taking them beyond simple questionnaire formats into more sustained and effective explorations of views on park development.

◆ In the case of those groups who wish to establish and manage areas within parks such as small woodlands or ponds, there may be a need to modify maintenance contracts.

Contact: Michele Wood,
Community Development Officer, Parks
Bristol City Council,
Leisure Services, Colston House,
Colston Street, Bristol BS1 5AQ
Tel: 0117 922 3753

3.3 Parks strategy:

London Borough of Bromley

Key themes
◆ Parks strategy
◆ Consultation
◆ Multi-disciplinary teams

Overview

The success of Bromley's parks strategy stems from the way it chimed in with wider corporate objectives. Good parks and open spaces are seen by the borough to be a material factor in creating a high quality of urban life and they are central to the long-term success of Bromley.

The adoption of the strategy has brought significant changes to both day-to-day maintenance of the parks and their long-term development. The strategy team looked closely at the needs and requirements of park-users, and how existing parks met, or did not meet, them. They then made changes in budget arrangements, staff roles and in the organisational culture within the parks service to help provision match identified needs. Standard specifications for all maintenance, planting and park furniture were replaced by tailor-made plans for each park, produced after careful research and evaluation. The key aspects of the strategy were:

◆ The allocation of existing funds to make fewer but more effective financial interventions;

◆ A rolling programme which allowed for investment and intensive management in one area of the borough at a time;

◆ Understanding people's requirements through market research and public consultation;

◆ The recognition that different types of parks require different types of management.

Ten years ago

In the past managers were confined to day-to-day supervision of grounds maintenance.

Financial management was carried out in the Chief Executive's Department and divorced from the daily managerial responsibility of parks. Park managers lacked good quality management information and were constrained by the inflexibility of grounds maintenance work practices. For Bromley, the positive side of the introduction of CCT was that park managers could begin to shape maintenance programmes according to the needs of individual parks.

At the same time, park budgets were reduced and the savings from CCT were applied elsewhere in the authority. Full-time staff were retained in the five most popular parks, the remaining 100 were covered by mobile staff. Although managers could now manage more effectively and respond to users needs, they had fewer resources to achieve high standards or to increase staffing levels.

The process of change

A "quality management programme" which was pioneered in the council by the Parks Service identified access, acceptability and awareness as critical factors leading to improved services. Adopting an enabling approach required a clearly stated set of objectives and standards to be met, and the spotlight fell on the need to define a good quality service. This approach was applied to parks management for the first time in 1992.

Bromley carried out market research in the form of focus groups, and developed a parks charter and an action plan. The consultation showed that people were concerned about security, especially for children. They wanted to see a return to some kind of park keeper system. There was little awareness of existing efforts to inform people about the parks through park signs and noticeboards, and existing leaflets were found to be confusing. Yet, the groups felt that in the main, the parks were well maintained.

Effective parks services

In 1992, the Leisure Services Committee approved a review of parks provision in the Borough. The Committee needed to have information upon which to make judgements and to defend parks service budgets, they needed to know whether "given resources and predominant users, is service provision effective?" Greater effectiveness depended on an approach to management and maintenance that was more sensitive to the needs of individual parks.

> *Parks are still very popular with people generally, but when it comes to a choice between competing priorities for public funds, parks will suffer...*
> DIRECTOR OF LEISURE & COMMUNITY SERVICES

One size doesn't fit all

The strategy development team began to consider how to define different kinds of parks. They had nine different types of parks and open spaces - parks, gardens, recreation grounds, woodlands, country parks, circular walks, golf courses, allotments, and dual use facilities. When they compared this with the GLC's, Greater London Development Plan (GLDP) which Bromley and most other London Boroughs had used as the basis for their Unitary Development plan, they found that its hierarchy of parks provision, based on size and catchment area, was a crucial limitation to the development of the parks. It took little account of differences in the quality of parks and open spaces, the varying uses made of them and the expectations people had of different kinds of parks. The GLDP approach, they argued, had been successful in protecting public parks from built development, but was no longer adequate as a framework for developing and managing the parks themselves.

They began by matching the range of uses that people make of a park (for example, relaxation, children's play, exercising dogs) with the basic characteristics of the parks themselves (such as physical features, accessibility, visual quality and diversity, costs and income) which produced a series

of further classifications. The findings led officers to produce six park types:

◆ Ornamental town park/garden;

◆ Multi-purpose park;

◆ Natural park/woodland;

◆ Sports grounds;

◆ Linear park/walk/ circular walk;

◆ Local open space.

The aim was to provide a range of parks in each locality which met different needs. The new classification allowed the parks team to make more sophisticated assessments of priorities for each park and how best to allocate necessary funds.

> *Clearly, not all parks can provide this broad range of benefits, but within a locality and given the often large number of spaces available (105 covering 2900 acres in Bromley), there should be a sufficient mix of park types to meet people's requirements.*
> DIRECTOR OF LEISURE & COMMUNITY SERVICES

Market research also picked up the success of some individual initiatives such as the borough walks. In developing new walking routes or re-establishing old rights of way, the parks team collaborated with local schools in clearing paths and way marking. The borough has sold 2000 local walking guides, an indication of the popularity of walks.

The beginning of a strategy

The parks team now had the basis of a strategy which was based on an acceptance that parks services had to find ways of defining success and failure, and that users' views had to inform park management. In retrospect, the parks staff now say that the change in their organisational culture, brought about by taking these points seriously, was the most important factor in the successful development of the parks strategy.

The pilot project

A crucial factor in Bromley's approach was to implement the strategy one stage at a time. It would have been impossible to try and introduce this approach to all the borough parks at once. They turned this constraint into an advantage and decided to pilot the strategy in one area of the borough. They chose the area around Orpington, which had a good mix of urban parks, local recreation grounds, sports grounds and a 'natural' park.

An audit of the area's parks

◆ Showed details on the size, access, the state of play facilities, the degree of vandalism, the events held in the park and a view of the deficiencies of the park and the opportunities to make improvements.

◆ Cross-referred this to an ecological survey and to the grounds maintenance review team who provided details on current contract work.

◆ Assessed the range of different parks available and whether they met the needs of local people.

Park managers could make decisions about whether the overall emphasis of a particular park should be changed in order to create a better balance of different types of park within the area.

> *One of the tools used for devising the strategy was the construction of a series of maps. A basic ordnance survey map of the pilot area was overlaid with separate transparencies showing each of the six open space types. Other information was added such as major roads, rail-lines, rights of way, play areas, derelict land, shopping centres and their catchment areas. In this way a much richer pattern of the different kinds of open space in the pilot area was built up.*
> SENIOR PARKS STRATEGY OFFICER

Planning ahead

There were 41 parks in the pilot area, and 10 of these were chosen for development. Each was assigned a 'multi-disciplinary team' chosen from landscape designers, arboriculturists, parks patrol staff, countryside rangers, grounds maintenance staff, events staff with input from an ecologist. Each team had to manage their own budget, devise their own plan and consult with the public.

Finance

The pilot strategy work has been funded by an annual allocation of £200,000 'top-sliced' from the Minor Work and Improvements Revenue Budget of £514,000 (in 1994/95). This proved to be an effective way of using the fund, as more significant investment could be achieved in one area of the borough at a time rather than dispersing funds to little effect over the borough as a whole.

Assessment

A household survey was carried out around Poverest Park, as part of the research for this good practice study, by the Comedia research team. It showed a positive response to the improvements carried out in the park. The new play facilities, have proved to be particularly popular. Good maintenance, general cleanliness and the attractive wooded area were also mentioned as positive features. The survey showed that the park is well used, with 17% of respondents stating that they had visited the park that day, and 34% said they had visited the park in the last 7 days.

The strategy team have learned the value of:

◆ Listening to the public, through market research, public meetings, and discussions with relevant groups;

◆ Multi-disciplinary teams which led to comprehensive park management and gave individuals a much more purposeful context in which to work. The teams are responsible for all aspects of the park from budgets to public accountability;

◆ The learning process. As the strategy moves around the Borough the team can adapt and modify their approach. Other departments are affected: the planning section, for example, are willing to consider the new typology and what it might mean for the planning perspective on parks and open space;

◆ Targeting scarce resources on one area at a time. This has helped to reduce the task to a manageable size and allowed staff to concentrate on achieving results;

◆ Providing a clear framework for outside agencies and interests to get involved, in some cases generating extra income through partnership arrangements, grant-aid or planning gain. Delegated management to sports clubs has also freed resources within the core team;

◆ Looking at parks within a wider strategy, for instance town centre improvement schemes, pedestrianisation or shopping/ office developments which can help finance park improvements;

◆ Linking with other specialist programmes such as woodland management and ecology to develop these aspects of urban parks;

◆ Setting park development in the context of borough-wide campaigns such as 'Clean & Green', 'Landscape for Leisure' and 'Plant a Tree', to enhance these aspects of urban parks and open spaces, and to access additional funds. These campaigns have also been used to introduce projects on small areas of open space where local groups take over sites and convert them into wildlife areas.

Contact: Robbie Stoakes,
Director of Leisure & Community Services,
London Borough of Bromley,
Central Library, High Street,
Bromley, Kent BR1 1EX
Tel: 0181 460 9955

3.4 An arts centre without a roof:

Castle Park, Bristol

Key themes

- ◆ City-centre renewal
- ◆ Tourism
- ◆ Public art
- ◆ Multi-disciplinary teams

Castle Park in the centre of Bristol came about as a result of devastating bombing in 1940. A post-war attempt to landscape the site failed to come to fruition. The possibility of putting substantial money into improving this anonymous open space came about through the development of the adjoining Galleries shopping complex in Broadmead, funded by Norwich Union. An agreement was reached in December 1987 between the City and the developer that a temporary car-park of some 500 spaces could be established on Castle Park, in return for £1.4 million funding for the re-design and enhancement of the park.

In 1988 an inter-disciplinary team was set up led by the Parks Department with a landscape architect appointed as project manager. This was a new post funded from the project. The team consisted of: the landscape architect, an urban designer, an archaeologist and the community arts officer. Further players were brought in with the introduction of an interpretation team, with representation from the City Museum and Gallery. The archaeologist on the team provided a double function: knowledge of the site for the landscape designers and knowledge of the history for the interpreters.

The Castle Park Forum, a group of local people with an interest in the future of the park, together with the design team produced a brief for the refurbishment of the open space. The involvement of the Castle Park Forum with the City Council team was an attempt to respond to the wishes of the public. It meant that the process was protracted, but also it produced consensus and a good workable brief.

Appointment of Public Art Consultant

After one year a Public Art Consultant, Lesley Greene, was appointed. A major task for her was to develop a strategy for public art. Her role consisted of identifying suitable artists, arranging competitions, writing briefs, liaising with the different City Council departments involved in the scheme and local arts organisations, setting up collaborative projects and fund-raising. An important aspect of the artists' briefs was that their proposals should be site specific, which could involve reference to the history of the site.

Art in the park

The park officially opened in May 1993. By this time most of the landscaping and artworks were completed and a programme of temporary artworks and events had been set in motion. Although there are some sculptural works, much of the artwork is concerned with street furniture and functional pieces. Twenty-four artists or groups took part in the project.

Maintenance and vandalism

Artists' briefs required that they make their work as vandal proof as possible and easily maintained. In the two and a half years since the park was opened there has been vandalism, mostly graffiti, but surprisingly little of great consequence. This is particularly remarkable in regard to the play area which is fairly secluded with equipment made from wood.

Management

There are regular meetings between all the officers with responsibility for the park, however the management structure is likely to change with the new structuring of local authorities. The most likely scenario will be to have one manager for the site with control over events and landscape management.

Conclusions

Castle Park provides a popular green space, attractive to local workers, families and tourists. The inclusion of artwork as an integral part of the redevelopment was on a scale not previously undertaken by Bristol City Council and the value of public art commissions in enhancing the quality of the environment has been appreciated by urban designers who are encouraging its inclusion in other developments, both public and private, in the city.

The potential for using the park as a water link was seen as very important (the floating harbour runs alongside it). A landing-stage was built and water-borne transport is being encouraged between the railway station, the shopping centre, and the docks area with its art galleries, restaurants and museums. The park is not yet finished but further developments depend on the raising of more money. The proposed scheme to glaze the roof of the ruined St Peter's Church is one which will require a huge budget, but other smaller projects are more realistically achievable.

Castle Park serves many functions in Bristol's city centre - as a conventional park, a place to meet, a place to relax, a place to escape from the nearby busy shopping district, as an excellent children's playground, as an art gallery, as a tourist attraction, and as a public space that adds quality to the urban mix. Compared with many indoor facilities, the cost of providing Castle Park most certainly represents value for money as part of the leisure and tourism offered by the city to its residents and visitors.

Contact: Bernice Keith,
Heritage Estates Officer,
Ashton Court Visitors' Centre,
Ashton Court Estate,
Long Ashton, Bristol BS18 9JN
Tel: 0117 963 9174

A brochure describing the park and its artworks is available from the above on request.

3.5 Safer parks project:

Rossmere Park, Hartlepool

Key themes
◆ Partnership funding
◆ Community Involvement
◆ Training
◆ Safety
◆ Events

Rossmere Park pilot scheme

Rossmere Park is an area of four hectares in an urban residential area within easy walking distance of three primary schools and two comprehensive schools, located just a mile from Hartlepool town centre, and serving a catchment area with a population of 6,000. This project was developed to encourage the community to take ownership of the park in the face of seriously eroded standards of parks maintenance and renewal, which had resulted in low morale within the work-force as well as neglect and abandonment of the park by the local authority. This, combined with increasing levels of misuse, vandalism and anti-social behaviour discouraged the public from using the park, resulting in a downward spiral of despair and disillusionment. Starting from such a low base-line, and armed only with a small budget, the project co-ordinator, Marney Harris, describes what happened next, in a diary she wrote especially for this study.

Diary of a Year

6th January, 1994. I arrived in the Parks section of the Department of Economic Development and Leisure with the grand title of Safer Parks Co-ordinator. I was in post on a one year contract, to develop the Safer Parks Pilot Project in Hartlepool literally from scratch. There was me, the concept, Rossmere Park, the materials budget of £10,000 and twelve months. In addition, there was a commitment to spend the budget on materials for training, as my post was entirely funded by the Teesside Training and Enterprise Council, although I was

housed and employed by the Borough Council. My recent experience was as Community Landscape Designer and project leader for the Easington Colliery Community Link Scheme.

Making contact

The first month or so was spent talking to the area housing officer, the local youth leader, the police crime prevention officers, Contract Services horticultural managers, trainee supervisors, the TEC, the education department, the local church, residents associations, ward councillors and many more; making contacts, putting out feelers, following up leads and gaining support.

The snowdrop effect

As the base of contacts and interested parties broadened, it became time to get out in the park and do something, and bring all these people together. Winter is not a promising time for open air events but fortuitously a flyer for 'Snowdrops in the Green' from Landlife made its way onto my desk. These would be ready for harvesting after flowering and available for replanting. The launch day was duly set for early March and 10,000 snowdrops were ordered.

10th March, 1994. Snowdrop Day. The project was formally launched by the mayor and 250 school children from five different schools, including one for children with disabilities. Refreshments were donated by local small firms and served by the Mothers' Union at the local church hall. A group of local children had prepared badges for all those who took part. The bulbs were duly planted, with assistance from the county countryside warden, into ground prepared in advance by horticultural trainees. All interested parties were invited and most came and met each other on a truly enjoyable day.

Changing perceptions

18th April, 1994 . A public meeting to form a group of Friends of Rossmere Park (FRP) was arranged and locally advertised by posters, press coverage and by inviting individuals and organisations, such as nearby sheltered accommodation, residents associations, churches, and schools to whom the park and its welfare seemed relevant. Some of these had already expressed interest after the press campaign and snowdrop day. Initially these meetings were a forum for complaints and much venting of mostly justifiable grousing; raising the issues of intimidation, rowdyism, drinking and drugs use in the park as well as complaints about pot-holed paths, vandalised seats, and lack of colour and interest in the park planting.

Taking positive action - Parks Watch leaflet

16th May. Given the level of concern with security and misuse in the park, coupled with the obvious lack of recognition of the existing staff and security provision in the park, the newly formed FRP worked together with the police and the council's security sub-contractor to produce an awareness raising leaflet for local distribution. The nearest secondary school assisted in production, involving the Friends in direct contact with the school.

School video

Prior to the commencement of the Safer Parks Project the crime prevention group at Brierton, the closest secondary school, produced a video of excellent quality on Rossmere Park and its importance to the community. It concluded that the park should be valued and not given over to a minority of misusers. The video was produced entirely by the school with financial assistance and advice from Safer Cities and the police Crime Prevention Unit, who have subsequently used it in their promotions.

Environment Week - Green Detectives Day

20th May. A day of environmental educational games and activities for school groups in the park was undertaken in conjunction with the Countryside Warden. Both children and teachers enjoyed pond dipping, mirror walks, and mini-beast hunts. The day provided an interesting change from the school routine, while giving a wealth of material for further study in many subjects across the curriculum.

Basketball in Rossmere Park

1st June. One of the issues raised by the FRP was that young people in the locality need somewhere to go and something to do. The nearby youth centre and the church hall provide venues for organised and casual groups, but there is scope for more. The Friends also felt that providing for youth would go some way to redressing the balance of the perception that young people are trouble-makers. Sports development had contacted me to say that they had some basketball posts and rings which were surplus to requirements and could be available for the park. They had no budget to install them, but the training programme could easily take care of that. The posts were duly installed on the all-weather pitch in the park. The instant they were up there were youngsters using them.

However within a week or two the posts were badly damaged. I felt that the reason was that the specification of the posts had been too low. This point was ultimately proved, as the strengthened replacements stood the test and are still intact after over a year. So, the lesson learned was to be cautious of tempting free gifts, if they do not fit the needs.

Rossmere Park Carnival

10th August. This was a day that took much hard work, but that we all enjoyed. The FRP had settled into a regular group of ten to twelve individuals who met about once a month. They still depended very much on me to be chair and secretary, but they were cohesive and willing and committed and full of ideas. My job was more to contain their enthusiasm and try to keep a lid on their expectations to prevent disappointment and disillusionment. Their wish list had to be channelled into what was achievable. The Carnival idea emerged.

There were face-painters, mask and model-making, orienteering, games, pond-dipping and environmental activities, and the playbus and a bouncy castle. Local groups set up tombolas, bric-a-brac and cake stalls for fund-raising in tents provided for free by the Territorial Army. The St. John's Ambulance Brigade, the police and security were all there. Teas were served in the church hall. The day was a great success, and all the groups who had stalls were very pleased at the outcome and the opportunity to fund-raise. Many of the activities were free, so children didn't need to pay to join in and have fun.

November & December

A preliminary meeting was held with the new Cleveland Youth Outdoors Co-ordinator to discuss the development of an orienteering course in Rossmere Park. On the 13th December, in a bid to use the park all year round, an evening of carol singing in the park was arranged. Over 100 people joined in a candle-lit carol singing evening under the stars.

Another year

In 1995, an orienteering course was developed in the park and hundreds of schoolchildren have enjoyed it. Schools have been given packs so that this now permanent feature can be put to continual use. The park carnival, held in glorious August sunshine, was bigger and better than ever, with trapeze acts and stilt-walkers. There have been green detective days and the primary schools assisted by the trainees have planted 30,000 daffodils to create a Field of Hope to raise funds for Marie Curie Cancer Care. The bulb planting day was a major morale booster for everyone. The schoolchildren, the Friends and the trainees are all looking forward to the display the

daffodils will create in the spring and for years to follow. The feeling of achievement came from having worked so hard for a good cause and creating a permanent feature. Some funding for the project has been achieved under the Single Regeneration Budget, and further funding is being sought from the Training and Enterprise Council.

Success or failure?

The pilot scheme in Rossmere Park set out to attract park-users and 'crowd out crime'. Without sufficient resources to commission detailed research, what I am left with is a fairly subjective evaluation of the positive effect on the park which the project has undoubtedly had. Numbers of park-users attracted by events can be quoted, there are photographs of smiling faces and favourable press articles. Schoolchildren and residents have written letters of approval. The FRP will endorse the change in atmosphere in the park. People did not want to go there in 1993 and now they do. The park has been reclaimed for the community to use.

In an uncertain future, all of us can only hope that this success will be built on and absorbed into council policy. If the project continues, it must take on the management issues of objective evaluation. I know that the project has had a profound effect, but the tools to justify and prove this to funding bodies, committees and policy-makers are something which is essential.'
MARNEY HARRIS, DECEMBER 1995

Lessons from Hartlepool

- ◆ A committed individual is often indispensable to the success of these such difficult initiatives.

- ◆ The post was funded not from a traditional parks budget but by the local Training and Enterprise Council, a potential new source of funds for parks initiatives elsewhere.

- ◆ The worker quickly got in touch with all of the other agencies working in the community to win their advice and support.

- Active participation through events like Snowdrop Day, began to change people's attitudes to the space.

- The setting up of a Friends Group provided back-up support and moral support through difficult times.

- In the end, it is the community which will safeguard and care for the park, and community support is absolutely essential.

- A visible security presence was provided by a local security firm, contracted by the council, whose members were themselves active in the parks development programme.

- Local schools were targeted for park-based activities and their involvement through the school video and other forms of support, won the younger generation to a more positive attitude towards the park, and a sense of ownership.

- Inappropriate equipment was quickly vandalised; appropriate and heavily-used equipment was left alone.

- Establishing a calendar of events, including an annual carnival, makes the space meaningful and important once again.

- To date, parks departments have very little fund-raising experience. In an era of partnership and multi-agency funding, this has to change.

Contact: Marney Harris,
Safer Parks Co-ordinator,
Hartlepool Borough Council,
Civic Centre, Hartlepool,
Cleveland TS24 8AY
Tel: 01429 266522

3.6 Green Strategy:

London Borough of Hounslow

Key themes
- Parks strategy
- Environmental education

A key element of the Green Strategy is nature conservation, but a broad approach to landscape and outdoor recreation was adopted in order to provide a more cost effective approach to maintenance and management. The problems faced by parks include: isolation of open space, infill sites, outdated maintenance methods and diminishing parks usage; areas dominated by regularly mown grass and devoid of any landscape structure; air and noise pollution; and the peaks and troughs within the grounds maintenance calendar. The Green Strategy will address these problems and provide a more cost effective approach to landscape maintenance and management.

A major aim of the strategy is to update the design of parks in the borough, many of which were poorly designed and had changed little over the last few decades. The strategy recognises that in certain places formal and labour intensive landscapes are an essential part of the local environment and these need to be maintained. However, in other open spaces a more naturalistic approach is not only more appropriate but may also be far more cost effective.

Ten aims for the Green Strategy are identified including the:

- Identification of 'green chains' linking parks and open spaces throughout the borough;

- Identification of existing and potential areas of nature conservation interest;

- Drawing up of a design masterplan, management plans and implementation programmes for each area;

- Rationalisation of the grounds maintenance calendar to even out the high summer peaks and winter troughs.

Strategic open space chains

The strategy aims to strengthen the links between open spaces provided by the 'green chains', by commissioning major hard and soft landscaping works. Clear sign-posting and way-marking with a distinctive logo, together with interpretative literature, are to be used to create a sense of identity and cohesion in the mind of the public for each of the separate chains.

Parks

Each of the 50 parks in the borough is to be assessed according to a range of criteria including location, current use, individual landscape elements, historical connections, nature conservation interest, current maintenance methods and cost-effectiveness. After a period of public consultation, costed masterplans are to be developed for each park. The strategy envisages most parks comprising a well-furnished entrance courtyard; a theme garden; play provision; and a nature conservation area. In addition some parks will have sports pitches and pavilion provision.

Six basic types of treatment are envisaged :

- Intensive amenity grassland management - the intention of the Masterplans will be to reduce the amount of regularly mown grass (currently 85% of all parks) by creating areas of new planting and implementing meadow grass regimes.

- Intensive amenity planting - annual bedding in parks is scattered and costly. The aim will be to retain bedding in key areas only and to seek sponsorship for this.

- Extensive amenity planting - the masterplans aim to revitalise the parks by providing a "wider and properly designed range of theme gardens" e.g. magnolia garden, camelia garden, memorial garden, and to replace and extend the current shrub areas.

- Extensive woodland planting - this will comprise low-cost planting using young plant material to fulfil a number of aims including nature conservation, screening, a filter for air pollution, educational purposes and to a lesser extent noise attenuation.

- Ecological areas and management for nature conservation - the Masterplan for each park will outline proposals for the creation of new habitats, and 'wildlife corridors' will be created by linking the parks to strategic open spaces.

- Extensive grassland management - some areas of intensively managed grass will be cut once or twice per annum and their potential for nature conservation improved by introducing wild plants.

Other aspects of the borough's open space resource are also considered in the strategy:

- Roads - opportunities for tree and shrub-planting will be investigated, particularly along major roads, to improve the overall image of the borough, help screen traffic and noise from adjacent development and to reduce pollution.

- Housing - well-designed tree and shrub-planting will be used to reduce the area of grass and thus summer cutting peaks. Climbing plants will be used to soften the vertical faces of buildings.

- Education - in school grounds a rolling programme of landscape works and masterplans which will include substantial tree and shrub planting are to be implemented. Environmental education areas featuring a range of wildlife habitats will also form part of the masterplan for each area.

- Industrial and commercial areas - the Green Strategy is to be used to influence landscape schemes accompanying new development, ensuring that the type of treatment is appropriate to each individual location and its particular setting.

- Other areas - areas outside of public ownership are to be identified, where upgrading, even if purely in terms of the removal of eyesores, is seen as an essential element in improving the borough's environment.

The strategy in a wider context

In 1993 Hounslow produced their Environmental Charter which covers a number of environmental issues of importance to the borough and its residents. The Green Strategy clearly relates to the Charter and in particular to its Green Spaces section where a number of Strategy undertakings and initiatives are repeated as objectives. Putting the Green Strategy into this wider context enhances its credibility at both the local and borough wide levels and ensures that action on green space relates strongly to undertakings on other environmental issues.

Monitoring

The production of management plans, the inclusion in the Corporate Action Plan of specific targets, and general consultation ensures an element of monitoring. The familiarisation of staff in the aims and objectives of the Green Strategy and in particular the individual elements of the management plans also ensure that any failings or omissions are quickly spotted. However, there is no formal monitoring which systematically records whether or not management plan undertakings have been put into effect, or how successful they have been.

An issue which has come to light, through the process of evaluating the success or otherwise of the various initiatives, is the importance of the quality of the initial design. Some of the areas of extensive woodland planted early on are now having to be cleared as they obstruct important views and sight lines. Similarly, initial pathways that were too narrow, and unsettling for people, have had to be changed. Better design would have obviated the need for this work to be undertaken.

Financial implications

One of the aims of the Green Strategy has been to make parks management more cost effective. Whereas the maintenance of annual bedding plants would cost in the order of £100 per square metre, shrub planting costs only £25 per square metre and woodland areas about £2 per square metre. This has enabled resources to be better targeted, enabling smaller, more formal areas to be managed at the intensive levels they require whilst larger areas can be managed in a more naturalistic way.

The Green Strategy is implemented through a capital programme focused on each management plan. In its first year this was £84,000, but this figure has since diminished. Once the initial period of establishment and maintenance has been completed the management requirements are built into standard CCT contracts. Little outside money has been directly attracted to the Green Strategy, although SRB funding has been secured for the regeneration of the Brentford area of the borough, some of which is allocated for parks and open space. English Nature has grant-aided the development of school nature areas, and planning gain has been used to develop and upgrade other areas of open space, most successfully at Bedfont Country Park. In Chiswick Park, an Aids Trust has funded the development of a Memorial Garden.

Consultation and community involvement

Consultation has been an important element in the formulation and implementation of the Green Strategy. Councillor and officer involvement at an early stage has proved crucial to its overall success. In particular, cross departmental liaison and consultation between Landscape and Environmental Services and Parks and Promotions has been essential.

The parks service also works closely with the borough's planners particularly in respect of specific environmental programmes, such as the one for Brentford, where upgrading of the green spaces, including roadside verges, is seen as an essential part of overall environmental improvement.

The strategy was originally presented as a consultation document. As it has proceeded

into its implementation phase, consultations with the public, local organisations, Friends Groups and local ecological advisory committees, have proved invaluable in responding to local needs and feelings. In particular, in considering the redesign of school grounds the involvement of the schoolchildren has been very effective.

Every year an area in a specific park is selected for a community planting scheme and local residents are invited to participate. Trees and equipment are provided by the borough along with basic instructions.

Boston Manor Park is one of the borough's major open spaces and one of the first and largest of the Green Strategy sites. It comprises an historic area around an old manor house, the River Brent and Grand Union Canal and a newly created theme garden. Under-utilised open space was brought under the Green Strategy and, in 1989, planted up with native trees and shrubs creating a visual and ecological link with the existing green corridor which extends along the river and canal system.

A Customer Research Survey was carried out in the park in 1995. The survey revealed that only 13% of park-users were aware that a Green Strategy existed, and thus the great majority were unaware of why changes were taking place in the park. Only 1% of park-users had attended the public consultation meeting held on the implementation of the Green Strategy in the park. The survey revealed that there was clear support for a move away from traditional planting towards a more imaginative, ecologically interesting and modern approach. Overall the survey concluded that the Green Strategy was making a subconscious impact on people's perceptions and visions of the park, but making little impact in terms of its own identity. Recommendations included the promotion of the Green Strategy in the local press, a stronger promotion of interpretation within the area of Green Strategy implementation, and the extension of the wild flower and natural planting to other areas within the park.

At Inwood Park, one of the most central parks in the whole borough, two play areas have been developed, a theme garden planted on old tennis courts, and wildlife and conservation areas established. Other sports facilities, including a football pitch and multi-games court, have been retained. Dense planting of native trees and shrubs has been used to give the less formal areas of the park form and structure, and to create links with other areas. Elsewhere low growing shrubs have been used effectively to create areas of low maintenance ground cover. An area for barbecue and picnics has been set aside and the borough have supported a local group to run a toy library. Musical and children's events are used throughout the year to attract the public to the park, and to ensure its high profile locally.

Marketing

Pamphlets and leaflets have been or are being prepared to promote and market both the Strategy itself, and a number of the Green Chains, although this programme is by no means complete. The Green Strategy Officer admits that greater emphasis now needs to be put on explaining and interpreting the changes to park-users through the production of leaflets and clearer signs.

Conclusion

The Green Strategy set out to reassess the role of Hounslow's parks and to come up with solutions to the problem of declining standards of parks management. Ecological planting and management is a key part of the strategy and where it has been implemented appears to have been accepted by park-users. The formula of including in most parks a well-furnished entrance courtyard; a theme garden; play provision; and a nature conservation area, also seems to have succeeded and has enabled resources to be allocated to areas of greatest need whilst providing lower cost, but no less important, alternative forms of management elsewhere.

Contact: Alan Smith,
Green Strategy Officer,
London Borough of Hounslow, Civic Centre,
Lampton Lane, Hounslow, TW3 4DN
Tel: 0181 862 5862

3.7 Proposed new park and park refurbishment:

Hulme Regeneration, Manchester

Key themes
◆ Urban regeneration
◆ Consultation

The Hulme neighbourhood enjoys an outstanding strategic position, pressed hard up against Manchester city centre on flat land to the south-west. Ironically the attraction of this situation has been dulled considerably by the stigma of its reputation for social unrest, crime and ugly environment. This contributed to a sense of isolation, exacerbated by a highway infrastructure designed in the 1960s and 1970s to divert traffic around the edge of Hulme, on roads which were impermeable to pedestrian flows in and out of Hulme. The subways and narrow footbridges were never inviting, even when new, but dilapidation and a growing perception of probable assault had begun to discourage most people from using them at all. Only if this stigma and 'suffocation' is removed can regeneration be expected to achieve the economic re-growth normally associated with physical rebuilding.

A new flagship park

The notion of a public park for Hulme is more than just an increment in the emerging plan for a new public realm; it is the central generator and organising influence, believed by many to be the symbol of environmental quality by which the area will become known and valued.

It must be clearly understood that the plea was not for 'more green space'. Hulme had ample green space already but it was so fragmented, run-down and meaningless that it had a net detrimental effect. Despite deficiencies in the green space they were familiar with, the community was undaunted in its call for a 'park'. It was obvious that they still believed in the viability of the concept and, through a sustained consultation programme, it has become evident that they also have a vision of how their contemporary model would differ from its Victorian precursors.

The research and consultation work involved in realising such a vision has been commissioned and co-ordinated by Hulme Regeneration Ltd. It began with an open space audit, carried out by Camlin Lonsdale, in which all green space throughout Hulme was surveyed and evaluated. Recommendations were made for conservation, refurbishment or conversion of each open space. Potential roles were identified for open spaces within the redevelopment and how they might connect with other elements of the existing and proposed public realm, especially those elements capable of 'darning' Hulme back into the surrounding city 'fabric'.

A network of robust urban spaces

The major output of the audit was the identification of good practice principles for the planning of open space within the urban design process for Hulme, governing scale, proportion, interconnection and dedication to residential property. The theories were based on real examples of city 'fragments' which have survived relatively well in Hulme and the surrounding areas.

It was possible to put these principles into practice at a crucial stage in the preparation of an overall plan for Hulme when Bellway Homes co-ordinated their urban masterplanning for redevelopment of the Crescents (high-rise housing) with the new park feasibility study, commissioned simultaneously by Hulme Regeneration.

Park principles
◆ The park should meet the main high street (the reopened Stretford Road, which had been pedestrianised when the Crescents were built in about 1970) at or near to the main centre. The motive here is to ensure that the park's existence is readily discovered by people passing through Hulme and to infer that its status is equal to that of other land uses.

- Where it meets the high street the park should assume 'civic' properties, ideally with a hard 'square' suitable for all-weather use.

- The park should seek to establish a new connection to Castlefield and the city centre, over or under the Mancunian Way dual-carriageway road which separates Hulme from the city centre. This would open up movement into and out of Hulme, from which the park itself would benefit.

- A mix of buildings, with a preponderance of houses, should present their fronts to the park to ensure overlooking at most times of day or night.

- Edges of the park should be as permeable as possible, visually and for pedestrians, but exclude vehicles. This represents a diversification of approach from the tradition of walls and railings and calls for design innovation to achieve the required 'filtering', especially if disabled access is to be maintained throughout, whilst still achieving bold and legible boundaries which people will recognise as containing a park.

- A clear visual and physical relationship should be achieved with movement routes through and around Hulme, using the park either to 'contain' one side of a road or as the stop on the end of vistas. This exploits the park as a profoundly effective aid to orientation and builds up a map of distinctive places.

- Artificial lighting should be used to avoid areas of darkness in the park. Particular consideration should be given to pedestrian or cycle routes which pass through the park to provide strategic connections.

- Developments within the park to provide for a wide range of recreation activities and include high quality sensory experience.

It will be observed that the majority of this list relates to the elements which form and locate the park rather than what appears in it. This is no accident and has two main reasons:

- If the facilities of a park are not protected and properly presented in a high quality container they are less likely to be valued and will deteriorate. The analogy of a chocolate box has been used: a present of expensive chocolates, lovingly wrapped in a beautiful box, is more likely to be appreciated and savoured than if handed over loose .

- Profound changes in patterns of social behaviour mean that park-visits no longer take place in the form of a 'day out'. If a new park is to be valued as part of the much more mobile contemporary lifestyle it must be 'thrust' into people's consciousness. As a consequence of its siting and integration with other elements of the public realm, Hulme's new park will be 'encountered' in the course of many journeys, especially those on foot, between home and shops or work and moving into and out of Hulme.

A park for the people, by the people

Hulme Regeneration Ltd have included consideration of the new park in several participative exercises. The policy has been to combine debate about the park with other strands of the urban regeneration, in order to help the community recognise the need for an integrated approach.

Community events such as a successful planning weekend served as a valuable focus for public participation and the process is to be sustained on an ongoing basis throughout the regeneration period. In order to fuel and manage this process the City Challenge regime provides for the establishment and funding of an organisation known as Hulme Tenants Participation Project (HTPP). It has a small number of paid workers and is steered by representatives of both the tenants and the City Council. During the course of the feasibility study for the new park, liaison took place through HTPP with as many residents of Hulme as possible. HTPP's advice was to conduct a series of design workshops, for the benefit of each of Hulme's neighbourhoods. Feedback from these area workshops was incorporated into the feasibility study report and then the

overall conclusions reported back to a final plenary public meeting for the whole of Hulme.

Delivering the vision

It is not envisaged that the public sector will deliver the entire park project, nor necessarily take ultimate responsibility for all of its management. The notion of a community development trust being set up within the Hulme community was well received during the consultation stage of the feasibility study, although no political decision has yet been made on this issue. This model assumes the rudimentary infrastructure of the park being taken over as a developing project by a trust with a high level of community involvement.

If this approach is adopted, the final design of the park can be expected to emerge only when such an organisation is in place and able to determine more accurately what funding will be available and what purpose each development within the park should serve for the benefit of the community. This has been described as a 'serial garden' approach, within which individual gardens or projects within the park would emerge as episodes in a long-term serial. The approach lends itself particularly well to the notion of recycling and sustainability for which there is considerable support and enthusiasm within the present population of Hulme.

Testing the principles: Barracks Park

Within the City Challenge area an opportunity existed for many of the design principles to be put to the test in a shorter timescale than is achievable in the new park. An existing community park, known officially as St. George's and locally as Barracks, was suffering all of the familiar symptoms of a neglected old park. However, there was enormous strength of feeling within the St. George's community against any suggestion of abandoning the park for development of any other kind. These feelings became evident in the course of design workshops arranged and led by Camlin Lonsdale, held within the community before any drawings were done. It is worth recording a number of

detailed procedures which have proved popular with residents on this and other participation exercises:

Encouraging participation

◆ Hold all meetings in community buildings near the site.

◆ Additional meetings with youth clubs and at school assemblies in order not to exclude any age group.

◆ Supplementary one-to-one discussion with people walking in or near the park, including children playing in streets nearby.

◆ Leaflet all properties and publish press notices also.

◆ Open discussion with pictures of the park as it is now and exchange opinions about its good and bad points, memories of how it used to be and ideas for how it might change.

◆ Report back to subsequent meeting with a synthesis of all early discussions and present a preliminary concept in the form of 'principles' and one or more ways of interpreting them. Use response to this as final design brief.

◆ Report back again with fully developed design proposal and be prepared to change it.

◆ In all sessions give the audience the choice of open or more intimate discussion.

◆ Listen more than talk.

◆ Ensure discussion is not dominated by select few.

◆ Steer discussion in a positive direction and on the subject but take note of significant concerns about unrelated matters, advising where such matters are more appropriately dealt with.

◆ If possible, establish core group of locals who are sufficiently committed to help organise further events, disseminate information etc.

◆ Distinguish between the interests of park-users and residents living directly overlooking the park.

Portrait of a park

The St. George's discussions proved to be very fruitful and a good picture of the park's past, present and future emerged. Consensus was reached fairly readily, with principles being agreed along lines fundamentally similar to those for the new park. This suggests that there may be contemporary themes common to many communities' aspirations for public parks which can only emerge from behind the sentimentality when objective debate is focused on a specific site.

A phased strategy for regenerating 'Barracks' park was adopted, investment priority being given to establishing a high quality, legible boundary treatment, with distinctive 'gateway' entrances capable of filtering access to exclude vehicular trespass. All entrances were designed to be visually permeable to the street and paths were reorganised to conform to a clear geometry with excellent sight-lines. One main north/south path and another east/west path were illuminated to approximately 20 lux average.

Lessons to be learned

Weighing against positive general response to the improvements there have been a small number of set-backs. At the risk of making them appear out of proportion there is value in analysing these set-backs in some detail in order to extract the lessons necessary to inform best practice.

Occasional vandalism appears to be a symptom of a general problem which seeks out unattended locations. Despite this, the most heavily trafficked parts of the park seem to suffer little, suggesting that if one can stimulate greater population of the park it will inhibit crime spontaneously.

Problems with a new pond were the freak consequence of development on another site, where a protest by conservationists led to a search for an alternative home for a pond and its contents. The whole was transported to Barracks Park, with hastily conducted consultations, which have failed to convince the St. George's residents of the wisdom involved.

The regeneration of Hulme is still at a relatively early stage but it is gathering momentum and media attention at a remarkable rate. Mistakes are inevitable during periods of great activity but lessons and wisdom are to be found in mistakes, so those responsible for the regeneration are setting aside the time and conviction to monitor progress and analyse both success and failure.

Contact: Hulme Regeneration Ltd, Brierfields, Boundary Lane, Hulme, Manchester M15 6EB
Tel: 0161 226 2323

3.8 Milton Keynes Parks Trust

Key themes
◆ Management by Trust
◆ CCT
◆ Monitoring and marketing

The Milton Keynes Parks Trust was established in 1990 to take over the funding and management of many of the town's parks and open spaces from the Milton Keynes Development Corporation, then in the process of being wound up. There had been some discussion as to whether it was best just to hand over the parks to the local authority, but as the local authority could not guarantee to ring-fence and maintain the level of spending on parks, the Development Corporation opted to set up a trust (with an endowment fund), to manage the parks after its demise. This decision still remains contentious with some local people.

The board of the trust contains a mixture of nominated members representing many of the main interest groups which would naturally have an interest in the quality and management of local green open space, including the Bucks, Berks and Oxon Naturalist Trust, the Royal Forestry Society, the Royal Agricultural Society, three nominations from the local authority, from the parish councils, from the local chamber of commerce and the local sports council. All board members must live or work in Milton Keynes, and are subject to re-nomination or replacement every three years.

The work of the trust is funded out of income generated by a property portfolio which was given to the trust on its incorporation to cover the costs of managing and maintaining the trust's 4,000 acres of parkland, parkways and the commercial property portfolio. The trust employs some twenty staff including secretarial, administrative, rangers, landscape officers, with a senior management team made up of the Landscape & Forestry Manager, the Parks & Estates Manager, the Finance &

Administrative Manager and the Chief Executive. The Trust operates from a purpose-built headquarters in Campbell Park.

> *Actually quite a few staff earn less than their local authority counterparts, but the difference is more than made up in terms of motivation, team-work and job satisfaction that is common to most charities.*
> SENIOR OFFICER,
> MILTON KEYNES PARKS TRUST

The trust is free of the obligation to put maintenance work out to tender, as it is a private company, yet all maintenance work is done by outside contractors, a situation which everybody agrees continues to work well. Senior managers claim to work with a pool of about 25 different contractors, awarding 'six substantial contracts a year' in a three-year cycle. They have no worries even about allowing private contractors to maintain SSIs (Sites of Special Scientific Interest), for in their words, outside bodies can do any work 'as long as the specification is right and the monitoring of performance is professional'. There is a probationary scheme for new contractors, and over the years they have been 'trickle fed' to higher standards and larger contracts by the trust, which it is probably better able to do than many local authorities, due to continuity of staff and having a dedicated team of rangers and landscape officers who monitor and control the quality of the maintenance.

> *Some contractors get very attached to particular sites and feel a strong sense of ownership of them, so much so that if they lose the contract, they feel quite upset, and not just about the money.*
> SENIOR OFFICER,
> MILTON KEYNES PARKS TRUST

There is a regular programme of events in the parks managed by the trust, including the annual One World - One Earth Weekend Festival held every year in Campbell Park which attracted more than 7,000 people in 1995; sell-out performances of 'Romeo and Juliet' in a circus tent on the 'Events Plateau' in Campbell Park; a series of Summer Sundays in a number of parks involving music, sports, arts and crafts; and many guided walks and events to do with local wildlife. Local people are involved in the management and maintenance of some aspects of the parks through volunteer conservation schemes, as the trust sees 'voluntary activity as a major part of our work', working closely with the local BTCV .

Accountability

The Milton Keynes Parks Trust is obviously conscious of a need to demonstrate local accountability - given that it is not part of the elected local authority structure - and it would claim to do this through close contact with the public through the ranger service, and through undertaking annual visitor research, which is then used to inform policy. The parks managed by the trust are best described as 'country parks', or large landscaped areas within the town, with leisure and sports facilities.

Milton Keynes Parks Visitor Survey 1995

The survey is based on a sample of 1200 interviews conducted with visitors to four different parks in June and August.
The main findings were:

◆ 75% of respondents lived within Milton Keynes;

◆ 50% of respondents claimed to visit once or twice a week or more often (23% on a daily basis);

◆ 50% travelled to the park by car and 30% on foot;

◆ the 3 main reasons for visiting in order of popularity were: taking a walk, bringing children out, walking a dog;

◆ although the sample of disabled people was small (4%), disabled visitors made more critical comments than most, and it is felt that more consultation is needed with disability' groups.

The Trust has recently decided to establish a network of focus groups in Milton Keynes to provide additional information and act as a sounding board for local opinion, with regard to park provision.

It is clear that parks provision in Milton Keynes benefits from having a dedicated agency working solely to a single remit, without having constantly to fight political battles for resources with other, equally important, local services, or follow the occasional vagaries of national and local political decision-making. Yet ironically, a majority of Milton Keynes residents are unaware that the parks are run by a trust and assume them to be just another local authority service. Equally interesting is the lack of concern by trust staff that this is the case, for as one of them stated:

> *We are not over-worried about whether the public knows it is us that run the parks or the local council. The important thing is that the customers think that the parks are run well, and enjoy using them.*
> SENIOR OFFICER,
> MILTON KEYNES PARKS TRUST

To the outsider, the overwhelming benefit which derives from owning, managing and funding a new parks portfolio as a dedicated trust is the continuity of staff, the single-mindedness of the organisational ethos, and the close attention to the job in hand. However new organisations, enjoying special status, and with fairly safe-guarded funding, will always enjoy advantages over long established, institutionalised, but democratically accountable municipal departments. But Milton Keynes is an unusual town, with a completely different portfolio of green open space to most other places of a similar size, with their more historic network of neighbourhood parks, formal gardens and recreation grounds, and so cannot be easily compared. The Milton Keynes Parks Trust is a brave experiment that clearly works, but the issues facing parks departments in Britain's hundreds of local authorities are often quite different and may often require different solutions, although there is much to learn from the Trust's commitment, vision and enterprise.

In summary, the service shows the value of:

◆ Continuity of staff and organisational ethos

◆ Successful development of portfolio of private contractors and clear contract specifications

◆ Publishing annual report and conducting annual visitor surveys

Contact: Ian Richardson,

Parks & Estates Manager,

Milton Keynes Parks Trust,

1300 Silbury Boulevard, Campbell Park,

Milton Keynes, MK9 4AD

Tel: 01908 233600

Fax: 01908 233601

Useful documents available from the Trust: Annual Report 1995 (£1); Conditions of Contract and Specifications for Landscape Maintenance by Term Contract (£20); Park Visitor Survey 1995 (£10).

3.9 Morden Hall Park:

The National Trust

Key themes

◆ Management by The National Trust

◆ Income generation

◆ Permanent staff on site

◆ Volunteer involvement

Morden Hall Park in Merton, South London is one of the few urban parks owned and run by The National Trust. As a Trust property, with the capacity to raise income from property and to maintain staff on site, the park is atypical and is not presented as a model for local authorities. However, there are useful observations to be made about the Trust's approach to park management and its combination of conservation with the development of commercial and community facilities.

The 125 acre park at Morden Hall is a mix of meadow land, old marshland, woodland and formal garden areas. The park has special conservation value. Over the last 80 years almost no pesticides or agri-chemicals have been used on the land. A recent grass survey showed that the meadow land now supports a very broad range of plant species. The hay meadows are cut once a year to allow flowers to seed and butterflies to complete their life-cycle.

The development of the site

Unlike many other National Trust sites, no charge is made for access to the park as the donor had requested that the park should be accessible to the public free of charge. The Trust had to find other ways of creating income. In 1992, the nursery buildings within the walled garden became vacant. The Trust approached several garden centre companies and asked for proposals for investing in the site. The arrangement finally agreed with a private company involved:

◆ An investment by the company to build the garden centre and to carry out a programme of restoration;

◆ Building the shell of the café and shop (the interior was fitted by the Trust);

◆ Providing and maintaining the car-park;

◆ Being responsible for maintaining the historic nursery-garden walls. In return the company was awarded a long lease.

The development of the garden centre and café created the momentum for the restoration of the park. The buildings provided a focal point for people and for further activity, as well as supplying regular income for the benefit of park. They have also paved the way for re-establishing a use for Morden Hall itself.

Trust status

Morden Hall Park has special Trust Status allowing any surplus of operating income to be spent directly on projects at Morden Hall Park. The park's income is raised mainly from the rental of property and leases:

◆ Registry Office, London Borough of Merton (rent)

◆ Private houses (rented out at market rates)

◆ Capital Gardens garden centre (annual contribution)

◆ Café and shop, National Trust Enterprise Unit (all profit)

◆ Craft businesses (rent)

◆ Grazing paddocks (rent).

Other income is raised from an annual craft fair. The park also receives donations from individuals and groups.

Staffing

The park is managed by the head warden and two full-time wardens. The three staff live on site and are responsible for the bulk of land management and maintenance work. The Environmental Education Officer and Café/Shop staff also assist with the management of the site.

The presence of full-time staff on site is crucial to the success of the park. The head warden acts as a linchpin and much of what happens on the site can only work because he plays a key co-ordinating role. He:

◆ Is the public face of the park, and is the point of contact for many outside organisations and individuals;

◆ Is known as a local expert on conservation issues;

◆ Is called on to provide conservation advice in other areas in the locality;

◆ Provides training for volunteers;

◆ Is responsible for the complete day-to-day management of every aspect of the estate including the properties;

◆ And the other two wardens help to maintain a sense of safety and security in the park.

The head warden is trained in countryside management and therefore is well placed to oversee the long term conservation of the site and to manage other staff and volunteers. However, since the park gains its income from the properties it houses, property management has become an important element of the management of the site as a whole.

Voluntary sector

The park has good connections with the voluntary sector in the Morden area, and in fact now has as much volunteer input as the staff can manage. It is also used by Community Services who, once a week, bring a group of probationers to carry out work in the park.

The London Wildlife Trust visit the park regularly to carry out conservation projects. The local Volunteer Bureau also refers individual volunteers to the park. The park currently has two regular volunteers, one of whom works for 2 days a week, the other for a couple of hours twice a week. Their work is closely supervised by the head warden. The volunteers feel that the opportunity to work in the park and carry out tasks has taught them much about conservation and provided them with new skills and insights.

Park use

The Trust has not carried out formal user surveys, although the evidence they do have indicates that the majority of park-users are local. In the summer most of the family picnics happen on an area of short grass close to the river and near the central core of estate buildings. The more remote long grass areas are more likely to be used by the high numbers of dog-walkers who visit the park. In the long-term, the park managers may wish to consider how best to make more of the park more accessible to people other than dog-owners. The half-mile pathway between the café and the city farm is an especially important link. The path needs to be secure and attractive in order to encourage cross-use between farm and park.

Education

The park has an educational resource centre staffed by an Environmental Education Officer, a post funded by the Trust. Sessions on environmental issues, local history, technology and ecology are charged at £60 a day or £35 per half-day for a class of children. The Trust intends to increase its educational role and extend it to a wider range of age groups. The education centre is seen by the Trust as important in the long-term role for the park in the locality as well as providing a place that specialises in conservation education.

Garden centre

The Morden Hall garden centre is inside the historic walled-garden on the site of the estate's old and derelict nursery buildings and is the first garden centre to be leased on National Trust land. It is independently run by a private company. A proportion of the garden centre's profit contributes to the maintenance of the park. The garden centre is also responsible for maintaining the car park which has space for 300 cars. The synergy between the park, the café and the garden centre is beginning to work well.

Café & Shop

The shop and tea-rooms are run by the National Trust Enterprises Ltd, employing 20 staff. The café opened in November, 1991. It is open daily all year seating a maximum of 75 people. The profit made by both the shop and the café goes back to maintaining the park. In 1994 they contributed approximately £60,000 to the running of the park.

Craft businesses

The old stables and potting sheds are now used as workshops for small craft businesses. The workshops are used by wood turning, furniture restoration and stained glass window businesses. The workshops are rented from the Trust who impose fairly stringent rules that ensure that the tenants do not alter the interior of the workshops.

The Registry Office

At one time most of the buildings in the park were leased to the council. The Registry Office is the only one left. The office deals with 1000 weddings a year, being particularly popular because of its location in the park.

City farm

Deen City Farm is an example of a partnership between the National Trust, Merton Borough Council and the City Farm - an independent community organisation. The farm was established 12 years ago and is supported with a grant from Merton Borough Council. It was relocated from the Phipps Bridge Estate as part of the extensive refurbishment of that estate and an entirely new farm has been built by the London Borough of Merton on an area within Morden Hall Park. The Trust have leased the land to the council for a nominal fee. The farm is open to the public every day of the week, attracting many volunteers who take part in every aspect of the farm maintenance and management.

Summary

Morden Hall Park is one of the few National Trust properties in an urban area. The majority of the park-users are local residents. Over the last five years, the Trust has sought to develop the park in the context of its urban environment. The conservation of the park is the priority and it provides a unifying theme to all those involved in the park from the commercial enterprises to the volunteers. The atmosphere created within the park is one of the care and maintenance of a historic and ecologically valuable landscape to which the Trust ensure public access.

In pursuing this aim, the Trust has involved many local groups and individuals, but they are not driven by community demands for example, from residents associations or residents in the borough. The Trust is not accountable to local people or tied to local political structures in the same way that most local authority parks are.

It is clear that Morden Hall Park, although open to the public, is not public land in the same sense that commons and some public parks are. It has a strong identity as a National Trust park. Some local residents do harbour resentment of Trust management of what they see as open space bequeathed to local people. The management of this kind of conflict is relatively unusual for the National Trust and as one of the largest and potentially the most influential land-owning conservation organisation in the country it has much to learn from urban experience at Morden Hall Park.

The key elements of success are:

◆ A manager and staff on site;
◆ The financial control and the capacity to use the properties to generate income for the park;
◆ The synergy created between the different businesses in the park;
◆ The clarity of vision or rationale for the park;
◆ The involvement of volunteers;
◆ The link with local history groups, conservation groups and local business;
◆ The good reputation of the Trust itself and its insistence on high standards.

The Trust still has to cope with and manage the conflict of uses, in particular:

◆ Overcoming the image it has with certain groups that it is an imposed landowner on public land;

◆ Finding ways of including different sections of the community, apart from those who already have a conservation interest;

◆ Opening up more of the park for informal use other than dog-walking.

Over the last six years, Morden Hall has changed from an under-used park to one that supports several different concerns. More than 50 people now work in the various facilities, businesses and offices within the park. The synergy between the café, garden centre and the park has worked to bring many more people into the park and provided a solid base for further development. The requirement to manage property in order to maximise income to the park demonstrates the ever expanding range of skills now demanded of staff in the management of, in this instance, a complex site comprising several very different facilities as well as housing and land management.

Contacts:

David Jenkins,
Managing Agent, The National Trust,
Southern Region, Polesden Lacey,
Dorking, Surrey RH5 6BD
Tel: 01372 453401

Paul Rutter,
Head Warden, Morden Hall Park,
Mill Cottage, Morden SM4 5JD
Tel: 0181 648 1845

3.10 Community development in Walsall's parks

Key themes
◆ Community development
◆ New skills
◆ Volunteer involvement

Since 1989 Walsall Metropolitan Borough Council Parks Division has attempted to involve local people in the management and development of the parks and open spaces. They began with the "Metro parks initiative" which included a major survey to find out about people's attitudes to the parks and what improvements were required. The surveys identified a need for park based projects and a partnership (with the Black Country Urban Forestry Unit and the Countryside Commission) was established to run an Urban Forestry In Public Parks project. A project officer was employed to extend urban forestry in parks and to run activities with local schools, clubs, youth groups and resident groups. This project alerted staff to the potential for much more community involvement in the parks and as a result, a Local Involvement Programme was established as a temporary project in 1995. The programme has now been adopted as part of mainstream parks development within the Parks division of Walsall Metropolitan Borough Council.

The Local Involvement Programme

The Local Involvement Programme (LIP) for parks aims to involve people in the management and development of parks and open spaces. The programme has been formalised as the 'development' side of park management, complementing and influencing contract management. It has also influenced the work of other departments and the Local Involvement Officer has a direct input into projects such as City Challenge Open Spaces project and the development of Neighbourhood Agenda 21 in Walsall. The key features of the LIP approach are consultation, partnership, promotion, voluntary involvement and the development of park management plans.

As a result of the various projects undertaken under the LIP, the staff throughout the parks service are more open to discussion with park-users and community organisations.

In Leamore Park, which was suffering from vandalism, it was widely assumed that any improvements would not last. The LIP officer opted for community development approach. He contacted youth clubs, the resident's organisations, the park action group, local schools, a young women's group, and the local family centre. These groups combined to set up a temporary park-based community arts project which ran successfully in the park and finished with a celebration event including a lantern lit procession through the park after dark. The project was considered to have been successful in focusing attention on the park and highlighting, in new and imaginative ways, concerns about the park and interest in improving it. The project also attracted grant aid from bodies such as West Midlands Art Board.

Consultation has been a major focus of all the projects carried out in the parks. More recently, officers have been working directly with friends groups and park action groups. They have set up mailing lists of people who wish to be involved in park projects. To date around 8,500 people have been contacted in the formal consultation exercises based on questionnaires and door to door surveys. However, the staff recognise the limits of formal questionnaires and have instigated various other approaches such as video projects with young people, and 'planning for real' projects. The circulation of simple leaflets and newsletters also provides a way of monitoring people's views and attitudes to development in the parks.

Palfrey Park

The council were approached by individual residents with complaints or comments about conflict and problems occurring in the park. The LIP team issued a newsletter and distributed 3000 copies to households around the park. The newsletter contained a questionnaire. 192 people responded and of these 101 supplied their name and address and asked to be kept informed. The LIP officer wrote to each one inviting them to a meeting at which the results of the survey were presented and ideas and opportunities for the park were to be discussed. Part of the display included invitations to become involved in the park, asking people:

◆ Can you help out with work to improve the conservation area?

◆ Can you help out with some play activities in the play area e.g. supervision or running events?

◆ Do you want to organise an event in the park?

◆ Do you want to help to organise sports coaching sessions?

◆ To help to protect the trees in the park;

◆ To assist with schools visits and activities;

◆ To help to research the history of the park.

Enough people filled in slips expressing their willingness to be involved to begin to organise a friends group.

Partnerships with local groups

The LIP officer and other parks staff have been catalysts in establishing several local groups who in different ways are involved in the re-vitalisation of the parks. Staff at all levels, including the community park wardens and the mobile security staff now offer their support to the friends and action groups.

For many local authorities including Walsall, the idea of working with community organisations to improve the management of parks is relatively new. No 'models' of good practice have yet emerged. However, there are lessons to learn from experiences to date. Two 'types' of community organisation have emerged in Walsall and elsewhere.

The first is a lobbying type group, which sees its role as voicing concerns and channelling complaints to council officers and to councillors. This approach is often a means to vent frustration and complaints about poor management practice. The confrontational nature of many of the exchanges between lobby groups and council staff can be exacerbated by defensiveness on the part of staff. The experience in Walsall has shown the importance of exploring shared aims and objectives as early as possible. This will help the authority and the group to work out short, medium and long-term objectives. The officers may well be able to address the immediate concerns and thus demonstrate a willingness and commitment to meeting the concerns of users.

The second type, is the group which sets out to take positive action, and if a council can support and match such initiatives then substantial joint gains can be made. These groups will look elsewhere within the community for support and will quickly make their presence felt to local councillors and local authority officers. They are likely to be willing to participate in events as well as setting up their own activities. In Walsall, officers working with such groups to agree long-term management plans for the parks are open with financial and management information, and, as far as possible, share the same aims as the group.

However, the trust and commitment of friends' groups can be sorely tested when a council is seen to fall down on seemingly simple tasks such as fixing potholes, replacing bins and benches. In Walsall's experience it is important to make sure that people responsible for such issues have contact with the friends' group and share the same objectives. Otherwise the whole project of community involvement can be quickly undermined.

Willenhall Memorial Park - Willenhall Friends Group (WFG)

Willenhall Memorial Park is a 50 acre park built on derelict land in the 1920s. During the last 15 years the park had declined and the full-time gardeners had been replaced by mobile teams. In 1993 a local friends group set itself up. The main concern of the group was to improve the children's playground and to re-establish full-time staff in the park. The council drew up a performance-based contract which allowed for a full-time gardener to be based there. The gardener is able to work directly with the WFG.

The WFG has been able to co-exist with other park user groups. The old boating lake in the park has been converted into a fishing lake and is managed by an Angling Club. The Angling Club and the council have a formal arrangement whereby the club manage the lake and in return collect membership fees and so on. As part of the arrangement the club is required to carry out coaching sessions for young anglers. The council consider the lake to be much better managed and stocked under this arrangement than it ever was under direct council management. The WFG has only been running for 18 months, but have been spurred on by their success. They have got a full-time gardener back in the park and a new playground. The angling lake is in good condition and the group suggest that the park is being used much more. The group intend to work with the authority to draw up a long-term management plan.

The success of the group depended on:

- ◆ Effort and commitment on the part of group members;

- ◆ Openness, honesty and optimism on the part of council officers;

- ◆ Early successes which helped to create momentum and give the group credibility;

- ◆ Direct contact with one or two key council officers: the presence of too many council officers present at friends group meetings can be counter-productive;

- ◆ Good relations with other park-user groups, for example with the fishing club and sports clubs;

- ◆ A good park to start with. A friends' group is more likely to be successful in a park that is generally seen to be a good

park. Such groups cannot be invested with magical powers to solve problems related to serious neglect, vandalism or social deprivation.

Youth Projects

The LIP team are currently developing three schemes with external agencies to set up detached youth workers to work in parks. Each scheme has been agreed with the local friends groups and community associations, who have been very involved in arguing the case for youth work. The youth worker will work alongside the Community Park Wardens and will undertake consultation with young people. In one park, the youth work will be funded in part by the National Association for the Care and Resettlement of Offenders (NACRO) and the City Challenge Community Safety Unit.

Volunteering

In their practical projects, the LIP team have also worked in partnership with several external organisations such as the BTCV. Together they have delivered a series of out of school activities for local children. The LIP project receives regular support from a number of volunteers. Several students have volunteered during holidays in return for assistance with dissertations and student projects. LIP provides training for volunteers as well as reimbursing basic expenses. To date the LIP project has relied very heavily on the support of one or two key volunteers. Between the 1st of April 1995, and November 1995 the project generated around 2,500 hours of voluntary input from 365 people.

Promotion

The various projects in the parks have regularly received coverage in the local press; the LIP project promotes its activities both locally and in the professional press. This is seen as an important part of its work. The project in Leamore Park was entered into the British Gas 'Working for Cities' award and finished in the top ten, and the video made by drama students was entered into the Times Educational Supplement Youth Action Award.

All over the country much of the news coverage of parks tends to highlight vandalism or decline. The team in Walsall have, wherever possible, tried to promote more positive stories of activities in the local parks in a deliberate attempt to counter the poor coverage parks generally receive. Staff have the skills to deal with the media, to write press releases and to produce good quality newsletters and leaflets to promote their activities.

Park plans

Various community events have led to agreement between community groups and parks staff to draw up plans for the development of the park. The groups agree a list of priorities that both the Council and the community groups can agree. They then work out costs, timetables and realistic deadlines. The Groundwork Trust has been contracted to help develop a community master plan which is to build on the projects recently carried out in Leamore Park.

The lessons from Walsall and the work of the Local Involvement Team are:

◆ Short-term projects are often a catalyst in helping new approaches to emerge. They bring new skills and enthusiasm to traditional service areas.

◆ Partnerships with the Urban Forestry Unit, the Wildlife Trust, BTCV, the Tourist Board and others help to bring in new ideas and allowed for voluntary involvement.

◆ The importance of promotion. The LIP staff are adept at producing simple newsletters and promoting events and activities in the parks to the local press.

◆ The ability to communicate and deal effectively with community organisations. In the past parks staff have not been used to community group meetings and public meetings.

◆ The need for creative thinking about fund-raising. Skills learnt from the voluntary sector have been very useful in putting together small-scale funding packages for park-based projects, both for capital projects and to support volunteer involvement.

To develop the programme the LIP unit needs to be able to offer community groups a wider range of expertise, particularly in areas of landscape design and ecological issues. The Local Improvement projects could also benefit from the overall direction provided by a wider strategy for parks and open spaces.

Contact: Ian Baggott,
Local Involvement Programme, Walsall MBC,
Leisure & Community Services, Civic Centre,
Darwall Street, Walsall WS1 1TZ
Tel: 01922 654012

3.11 Play provision in parks:

Stirling District Council

Key themes

◆ Children's play

◆ Community involvement

◆ Disability access

The Play Services Manager, Sue Gutteridge, is situated in the Department of Community Services, Stirling Council. The grounds maintenance section of this department had traditionally held the remit for playgrounds as part of their overall responsibility for parks. Under the provision of CCT, parks maintenance included playground maintenance. However, much of parks maintenance focused on horticultural provision and playground maintenance tended to be marginalised. The playgrounds (105 in all) were poorly served and in desperate need of regeneration by the time Sue Gutteridge was charged with their care.

Over the past four years she has set about re-designing and regenerating Stirling's play areas. This has been done through a combination of:

◆ Consultation with parents and children;

◆ Facilitating the ability of community groups to raise funds, manage and celebrate the play areas they have helped to develop.

Before any play area is re-designed, extensive consultation is undertaken with the people and residents most affected by change. The worker is in a prime position to do this because of contacts already made in Community Services and Children's Services. Colleagues already working in areas earmarked for redesign are contacted as a way into the community. Trust has already been established and can be developed to include people who may not have had contact with the council in this way before. Stirling District Council Play Services has responsibility for the whole range of children's play provision, including staffed play projects as well as public play areas, ensuring a child-centred rather than grounds maintenance approach to play.

Multi-use

In other instances, Sue Gutteridge has been approached by parents to assist in re-developing play areas. Waverley Park, for example, was dominated by a football club which was not resident in Stirling. The park was quite small and unable to sustain multi-use. Residents complained to the Council that their open space was hi-jacked by non-resident footballers. The footballers were offered an alternative site for their activities and consultation with the Waverley Park community began on what they wanted for the site.

The park now incorporates an original swing, a 3 metre moving, elongated snake, designed and decorated by local children in conjunction with an artist, a selection of equipment designed to develop motor skills and balancing, a sand pit, shelter for local young people who hang out at night, a kick-about area and trim equipment. Although the site is not overly landscaped, trees have been planted by locals to match a row of limes on the opposite side of the road. This will eventually provide a buffer to traffic. A commemorative tree has been planted at each entrance to celebrate the community input into the design and construction of the site.

The site itself is surrounded by a wooden fence to prevent dogs from entering. But added to this are a number of stiles over which children can climb to gain entry. Dog grids are positioned at each gateway entrance to deter dogs. Signage is prominent and does not discourage people from any activity except dog-walking. A direct telephone line is displayed to encourage people to report damage which can be dealt with immediately.

The site is overlooked by housing. Because of this and the initial involvement in design and construction, there is a strong sense of ownership of the park which ensures a sense of safety for children who frequent the park alone.

Accessible to all - integrating children with disabilities

All play areas are accessibly designed to integrate children with disabilities. One playground has incorporated equipment designed for children with cerebral palsy. A cerebral palsy unit is located nearby, and the children were consulted on preferences for play equipment. An exciting wooden teeter-totter which responds to wheelchair weight is an attraction for both children in wheelchairs and children on bicycles.

Although this is a successful design, Sue Gutteridge now believes that special equipment is not necessary for an integrated accessible playground. On-site carers and assistants are more relevant to the needs of children with disabilities. This assistance is available in the summer months when staffed play sessions are offered. All playgrounds are seen as opportunities for guardians and carers to socialise, and seating is arranged to ensure comfort and contact. All tables have room for wheelchair access, important not just for children but older carers as well.

No vandalism

There was no vandalism evident at any of the 12 sites visited. The consultation processes undertaken were different in each area according to the circumstances. In Plean, guardians and children were taken on trips to look at other play areas to give people a frame of reference of what could be done, and to look at their own children playing in a different context. In this way, guardians' memories of their childhood are not dismissed but rather brought up to date.

In Raploch, a relatively poor area of Stirling with recent but neglected play equipment in housing estates, extensive consultations were undertaken with children in schools.

They were asked what they did last night after school, and what they did last week, in order to gain a realistic picture of children's leisure habits. Stirling is surrounded by reasonably accessible countryside with exciting natural features. Almost all the older children, especially the boys, engaged with the natural environment as their play space. Many purpose-built but now derelict play areas were scorned: some were used in unintended ways, others used for social gathering places. These play areas were areas of abandonment and disappointment for children. They did not seek them out as destinations, but only engaged with them as a matter of last resort.

This is valuable information for planning play spaces and contrasts with other areas of consultation where solutions were relatively easy to implement.

A case for celebrations

As play areas are redeveloped in Stirling in collaboration with the local community, celebrations mark their opening. These are sometimes one-off and sometimes on-going annual events managed by the community in conjunction with the council.

Stirling Council's commitment to redeveloping its play areas is not simply dependent on policies or strategies forged by its officers. It is dependent on highly motivated staff who have the ability to think strategically and implement ideas on the basis of proven need. The grounds maintenance people now engage with play-users to discuss improvements in play provision - they are no longer just involved in maintenance. This informal arrangement has the benefit of keeping the worker in touch with play areas in a way that she could not do alone. She has enthused the staff with her vision and it is beginning to pay off.

However, she does not have responsibility for parks as a whole and as such the play areas again must be seen as still relatively tangential to parks. Unless play and parks go together, an holistic approach to children's play and the overall quality of outdoor provision for all is unable to be achieved.

Unitary authority

Stirling Council will become a Unitary Authority in 1996. Play Services will be transferred from Community Services to Education Services, and will become part of a comprehensive children's service. While Sue Gutteridge does not want play to be subsumed by educational imperatives, she sees an opportunity for play areas and school playgrounds to forge new partnerships in design and consultation.

Lessons from Stirling

◆ Play strategies must start from the needs of the child, not the local authority.

◆ A professional, dedicated children's play officer, with strategic powers, can implement change effectively.

◆ Consultation takes different forms for different situations.

◆ There is no reason why most children's play provision should not be accessible to children and carers with disabilities.

◆ Play provision directly related to housing provision can create a sense of local ownership.

◆ The more it is possible to devolve play budgets to local decision-making, the greater is the involvement from local people.

◆ Play provision can create occasions to celebrate local achievements and consolidate ownership.

Contact: Sue Gutteridge,
Play Services Manager,
Stirling District Council,
Beechwood House, St Ninians Road,
Stirling FK8 2AD
Tel: 01786 432358

3.12 Management of West Ham Park:

Corporation of London

Key themes

◆ Management by the Corporation of London

◆ Permanent staff on site

◆ Safety

West Ham Park in the London Borough of Newham covers seventy-seven acres. It offers a number of facilities to its visitors: extensive open stretches of grass containing two football and two cricket pitches, nine tennis courts, a flower-crammed ornamental garden and large and well-equipped playgrounds complete with paddling pool. It is a Corporation of London park and run along traditional lines with high levels of funding and staffing. What difference does this make, if any?

West Ham is a successful park: well-used, finely maintained and relaxed in atmosphere. Maybe West Ham Park works because it is run by a non-local body rather than working despite being run by a non-local body? Are there lessons to be learned from West Ham Park?

A different history and a different management culture

The park started out as the grounds for a stately home. In 1874, however, the estate owners sold it to the Corporation of London which undertook to care for the resulting public park in perpetuity. It was the first open space the Corporation acquired outside the City of London. That sense of an honoured pledge still hangs over the gardens today. West Ham Park is now a secure island in an area in which unemployment is high and health rates are low. In parks round about, standards have fallen with the recession; vandalism is a problem. West Ham Park is carefully maintained, locked up at night and patrolled by day-time by park-keepers. Six of them actually live in the park itself.

When trouble has threatened, the park management has acted decisively. When the café started to be frequented by so-called 'undesirables', it was closed. When an attendant was menaced by a young man with a knife more recently, the park was shut for two days, by which time the police had made an arrest. This firm style has very many supporters both inside and outside the park. 'There's a kind of old-fashioned attitude,' voiced one middle-aged man, 'And I say that approvingly. They expect standards and, for me, I'm pleased about that. They're not prepared to turn a blind eye to things that are going wrong.'

A group of five young Asian teenagers kicking around a ball stopped to consider what they thought about the park: 'Strict, but fair. You feel safe here,' they concurred.

Feeling safe

Feeling safe came up, time and again, as the great advantage of West Ham Park. Intimidatory older children are kept out of the playground, said a young woman. Bicycles, even if pushed, are forbidden in the park because of their capacity to harm walkers. The playground particularly underscores the sense of security: a large concrete space with a mass of different pieces of brightly coloured play equipment, it is completely closed in. To get either in or out, it is necessary to go through a single gate. And beside that gate is the playground attendants' house, with an unimpeded view of the entire playground through its large picture window.

Playgroup leaders appreciate the equipment, but it was again the safety of the space that they rated most. Because the attendants were so good, play leaders would even be happy to let 7 or 8 year olds go off into the park on their own: 'They chuck out the 17 or 18 year olds, and that's good. You feel a bit awkward, being with little kids when older ones are smoking and swearing away.'

What does West Ham offer?

According to local people, West Ham Park itself offers a number of distinctive benefits over and above borough parks:

◆ It is spacious and well maintained;

◆ It is generally safe from threat;

◆ It is particularly safe for children.

What are the reasons for West Ham Park's success? The first and obvious answer is that West Ham Park has access to far more money that any borough park. But money on its own cannot make a policy. It is what an organisation does with money that makes a policy.

Money for staffing

West Ham's funds are undoubtedly generous, in present-day terms. The park's net expenditure for 1995/6 is £718,700. This is just under half of Newham's total parks budget. The largest proportion in West Ham's budget goes to staffing - 44%.

It is both the quality and quantity of its staffing that appears to give West Ham Park its distinctive asset. In all, they employ 16 park-keepers and gardeners, and there are up to 5 keepers on duty at any one time. Many have been employed for a number of years, bringing continuity. At times of maximum usage (such as in the summer), they are augmented by relief staff and members of an outside security firm.

Vigilant watchful staff

'People pass other parks to get to this park,' said a park-keeper. 'Why? Because it's well-maintained, well supervised and well patrolled.'

However, there are times when members of the public feel that staff can over-react. 'I can't see anything wrong with a couple having a cuddle,' mused a man. A group of young Asians claimed they'd been told to stop playing cards at one of the picnic tables, and a young woman photographing the park was approached by an attendant and asked what she was doing. Some of the rulings seemed silly too: 'What's the point of saying we have to keep off the grass in the quiet garden?' asked a young woman, 'That's the best bit in the summer. It's just where you want to be.'

Beyond these small negotiations, West Ham Park does not have to deal with the public in a really fundamental way because the public is not its pay-master. The money for West Ham Park comes not from local rates and taxes but from an ancient property fund, administered by a Management Committee which meets five times a year. Critics will point to a total divorce from the feelings and affairs of local people and cite examples of park practice in support of their case.

◆ There is, for instance, no policy of allowing local groups to use the park for fetes, fairs or fund-raising events;

◆ The bike embargo particularly affects young children whose parents would not let them cycle in the streets;

◆ There are no refreshments beyond an ice-cream van parked outside the children's playground;

◆ There are few facilities for older children and teenagers, quintessentially seen as trouble. West Ham Park however has the capacity to set up sports courses and training courses specially geared to teenagers. Its park keepers have sufficient rapport with, and respect from, the young people to involve them in some planning for their own future;

◆ The horticultural energy goes overwhelmingly into the ornamental quiet garden. The park itself could be more scenically interesting.

The park and the locality

The park has no information on who comes there and from where, as well as who does not. Borough parks have an obligation to discover to whom they are catering, and to adapt their practice accordingly. There is no policy of reflecting local demography in the park's own staff, particularly those visible to the public, although the very low staff turnover may inhibit opportunities.

Freedom versus controls

West Ham Park, in conclusion, offers some conflicting lessons. The comparative freedom it enjoys from outside constraints can lead to an insensitivity to local populations and the substantial levels of staffing can lead to an over-protective, over-zealous approach.

But it is undoubtedly the case that the security of tenure and the general camaraderie allows staff to develop a strong identification with the park. It leads to significant customer satisfaction and an important feeling of personal safety. The old-fashioned, rather authoritarian approach reassures many users.

So West Ham Park does have lessons to offer:

◆ Freedom from local constraints can lead to a better service. However, it needs to be monitored in order to avoid the counter-danger of insensitivity;

◆ Staffing is of prime importance to the public in making them feel safer;

◆ Staff perform better and have more job satisfaction if they operate within a reinforcing team structure, if they can feel they can influence practice, and if they have the security of job continuity;

◆ Money is less important than job satisfaction and job security to members of staff;

◆ The ability of a park management to move quickly in responding to trouble reassures the public.

Contact: Stewart Reid,
West Ham Park Deputy Superintendent,
West Ham Park, Upton Lane,
London E7 9PU
Tel: 0181 472 3584

Supplementary Case-Studies

No	Case-study	Themes	Pages
3.13	Children's play area: Royal Victoria Park, Bath	*Children's play, tourism, staff on site.*	95
3.14	Management structure and play: Battersea Park, LB Wandsworth	*Individual park management plan, events, partnership funding.*	96
3.15	Draft parks strategy: Bedford BC	*Parks strategy, consultation, promotion.*	97
3.16	New parks as part of a city centre strategy: Birmingham CC	*City centre renewal, community involvement.*	98
3.17	Urban forestry in parks: National Urban Forestry Unit	*Partnership funding, community development, new skills.*	99
3.18	Community park: Bromley-by-Bow Centre	*Community trust management, partnership funding, community development.*	100
3.19	Parks initiatives: Calderdale MBC	*Income generation, site management, providing an infrastructure of parking/toilets/ refreshment, controlling dog use.*	101
3.20	Monitoring parks costs: Victoria Park, Cardiff	*Value for money, monitoring.*	102
3.21	Castlefield Urban Heritage Park, Manchester	*Urban regeneration, tourism, management company, partnership funding, new skills.*	104
3.22	Centre of the Earth, Birmingham	*Environmental education.*	105
3.23	Parks and the DSO: Cheltenham BC	*CCT contracts.*	106
3.24	One o'clock clubs and events in parks: LB Lambeth	*Children's play, buildings in parks.*	107
3.25	Cannon Hill Park, Birmingham	*Buildings in parks, events, providing an infrastructure of parking/toilets/refreshments.*	108
3.26	Visual arts co-ordinator for outdoor arts: LB Merton	*New skills, public art.*	109

No	Case-study	Themes	Page
3.27	Playgroups and nursery schools in parks: Mid-Sussex DC	Buildings in parks, children's play, integration of indoor & outdoor leisure.	110
3.28	Play strategy: North Hertfordshire DC	Children's play, disability access, consultation, parks strategy.	111
3.29	Parks and open spaces strategy and community development officer: LB Newham	Parks strategy.	111
3.30	DSO and parks maintenance: Oldham MBC	CCT Contracts.	113
3.31	Community Garden Project: Quaking Houses, Durham	Community Garden Community development, partnership funding.	113
3.32	Health and fitness development officer: Birmingham CC	New skills, health, link between indoor & outdoor leisure.	114
3.33	Nature conservation and BTCV: LB Richmond	CCT contract won by environmental group.	115
3.34	Parks ranger service: LB Southwark	New Skills - parks rangers.	116
3.35	Community involvement: St George's Gardens, LB Camden	Community involvement.	117
3.36	Urban ranger and countryside warden service: Stockport MBC	New skills, health.	117
3.37	Developing a service plan: Walsall Arboretum	Individual park management plan, charter mark.	118
3.38	Urban wildlife groups in parks: The Urban Wildlife Partnership	Community involvement, partnerships, environmental education.	120

3.13 Children's play area:

Royal Victoria Park, Bath

Key themes
- Children's play
- Permanent staff on site
- Tourism

The play area of Royal Victoria Park was re-designed, landscaped and furnished with new play equipment between October 1989 and April 1990. Previously the area had been used for play, but was flat, uninteresting, and much of the equipment did not comply with British Standards and was set over tarmac or concrete. Nevertheless, it was popular because of its position close to the city centre. For these reasons, and the fact that there was a very generous area available for development (1.6 hectares) it was decided to seize the opportunity to make something special and different with the space.

The budget for improvements was £140,000 which covered building, landscaping, the purchase of equipment and its installation. The design work was done in-house. Jonathan Peters, the officer with responsibility for the play area said: 'It has become a regional centre, and part of our intention to set it up as such was to attract people to the city.'

Design

Two main aims influenced the design: to create interest on a flat site by contouring the ground, and to divide the area up into different themed areas that would appeal to different age groups.

The five main sections of the play area comprise:

- 'Green Park Station' which uses multi-play-units in the form of trains with carriages and a platform and was inspired by Bath's station of that name;
- An area of tepees, horses and wagons which relates to Bath's American Museum;
- A mound with a climbing frame bridges and archways, and embankment slides, reminiscent of the Pulteney Bridge and Weir;

- A larger mound incorporating the more challenging equipment for older children, with cantilever swings, tube slides and a bridge. This area suffered from erosion because of heavy use, and timber stockade has now been introduced in the form of a maze, thus redirecting traffic and offering extra play value;
- There is also an area which has net climbers and a variety of swings, including some specifically designed for disabled children.

'Free' space

Between the areas of play equipment there are large spaces of grass where families picnic and ball games can be played. The area is surrounded by fencing to keep dogs out, and there are restrictions on cycling and skate-boarding.

Supervision

An attendant is on site 364 days a year from 8am to dusk. The play area is locked at all other times. The role of the attendant is to monitor what goes on in the park, to provide first aid and to be aware and helpful. The attendant also does some maintenance of the site such as raking sand and collecting litter.

Facilities

The attendant's room is situated alongside the toilet block which has separate toilets for children and adults. Two additional features are a commercially run bouncy castle and carousel and fairground equipment. There is also a refreshment stall which operates during the summer months, and an ice-cream van. These concessions are very popular with traders as the number of people using the area is so high.

Current situation

The playground has now been open for five years and is immensely popular. On a sunny Saturday it is packed. People travel from surrounding areas specifically to use this play area, and letters of appreciation from visitors from all parts of the country are not uncommon.

Conclusions

This very popular and imaginatively equipped play area is successful, but in danger of being overwhelmed by its own success. It does not take long for facilities to deteriorate and the current plan to use a relatively large sum for reinstatement works proves the commitment of the City Council to its continuing success. The demise of Avon County Council and the restructuring of the local authorities for Bristol and Bath will lead to a new management structure and changes in funding.

Lessons from Bath

The principal lesson to be learned from the success of the Victoria Park children's play area is that once you achieve a 'critical mass' of play provision the numbers of users become self-perpetuating (and therefore self-justifying). Families come from long distances and expect to spend a long time in the play area, so they bring picnics and it becomes a day out rather than a short 'trip to the swings'. The numbers of users also clearly justifies having paid attendants on duty throughout the year, and the playground gains a reputation for being safe and well looked after. The regional reputation of the local authority is obviously enhanced by the quality and success of the playground, and adds another feature to the list of Bath's visitor attractions.

Contact: Jonathan Peters,

Contract & Development Manager,

Bath City Council, Department of Leisure, Tourism & Economic Development,

Royal Victoria Park Nursery,

Marlborough Lane, Bath BA1 2NQ

Tel: 01225 448433

3.14 Management structure and plan:

Battersea Park

Key themes

◆ Individual park management plan
◆ Events
◆ Coherent landscape design strategy
◆ Partnership funding

Battersea Park in Wandsworth, London, is one of Britain's best known parks, over 200 acres in size, and receives more than 3 million visits a year. It contains large areas of historic landscaping, lakes, games pitches, a children's zoo, a Festival of Britain Garden, athletics ground, tennis courts, large hard-surfaced events site, an art gallery, and many walks and carriageways. It also has car-parking facilities on site for up to 1,000 vehicles.

The park is directly managed by Wandsworth Borough Council, and has an on-site Battersea Park Manager, with staff including:

◆ Events co-ordinator;
◆ Administrative officer;
◆ Technical and events manager;
◆ Children's zoo manager;
◆ Pump House manager (the art gallery).

In addition there are a number of engineers and technical staff, animal keepers, administrative assistants and labourers directly employed by the council. Security is provided by the Wandsworth Parks Police, managed by the council centrally.

Managing this large site, with its many different kinds of activities, is a complicated business, which succeeds, according to the chief parks officer, through having an integrated site-based management team. Grounds maintenance is provided by a private contractor.

For the team to work efficiently there has to be a management plan. Such a plan was developed as soon as Wandsworth Council took over the park on the abolition of the GLC (Greater London Council), and in 1995 was supplemented by a comprehensive 10 year Landscape Restoration Management Plan, with a view to securing additional funding from the Millennium, National Heritage Memorial Fund and Sports lottery funds. The plan was prepared in consultation with the Friends of Battersea Park, the borough planner, English Heritage and other bodies. It identifies potential funding partners for each stage; indeed the refurbishment plan itself will have its own project manager.

The lessons of integrated, site-based management employed here could easily apply to many parks elsewhere, particularly those aspiring to offer a wide range of activities for the whole family, where length of stay is reinforced by offering a range of quiet and busy places, contemplative and active recreation, with car parking, toilets and catering to back it up.

Contact: Mike Wilkinson,

Chief Parks Officer, Leisure & Amenity Services Department,

Wandsworth Borough Council,

The Town Hall, Wandsworth High Street, London SW18 2PU

Tel: 0181 871 6368

3.15 Draft parks strategy:
Bedford BC

Key themes
- ◆ Parks strategy
- ◆ Consultation
- ◆ Promotion

In September 1994 Bedford Borough Council published a Consultation Draft Parks Strategy for public debate. The clear and well written document setting out the policies on parks which the Council wishes to pursue were printed and distributed to 150 local individuals and organisations, seeking public comment.

The council's philosophy is summarised by reference to two key issues:

- ◆ That the council will move to a

management rather than a maintenance oriented approach to parks and green space which will redress the current perceived decline of the landscape and facilities.

- ◆ The need to create a much more pro-active approach to encourage the use of parks by the local community and the involvement of local people in the development and management of parks.

The draft strategy sets out six proposed policies, each with an action plan. They refer to:

- ◆ Issues of maintenance and refurbishment;
- ◆ Creating more varied landscapes;
- ◆ Encouraging greater community use of parks and green space and community involvement in management;
- ◆ Providing more information on facilities and activities;
- ◆ Exploring alternative methods of raising funds;
- ◆ Protecting existing parks and green space in the Local Plan.

Each proposed action is identified in terms of implications for council resources, thus:

0 Work is on-going

1 Achievable in the short-term with no additional resources (less than 3 years)

2 Achievable in the medium-term with no additional resources (less than 6 years)

3 Achievable in the long-term with no additional resources (more than 6 years)

4 Achievable only with additional resources

Public response to date has been positive, and the document is also a focus for discussions with local groups.

Contact: Stephen Tomlin,

Chief Amenities Officer,

Bedford Borough Council,

Development & Amenities, Town Hall,

St Paul's Square, Bedford MK40 1SJ

Tel: 01234 267422

Copies of the Bedford Draft Strategy can be obtained from the above officer at a cost of £5.

3.16 New parks as part of the city centre strategy:

Birmingham City Council

Key themes

◆ City centre renewal

◆ Community involvement

◆ Multi-disciplinary team

Two new parks - City Centre Gardens and St Thomas's Peace Gardens - have been established in the city centre of Birmingham. These new parks are part of the wider strategy for investment in open space in Birmingham City Centre, and demonstrate the role of the urban park as part of the plan for an integrated public realm - of streets, squares, canal side walks and green open space -that provided the backbone for one of the most significant redevelopments of a modern British city centre. As the city centre strategy work pointed out, there is no one major city centre park in Birmingham, instead the centre has a series of open spaces along pedestrian routes and other reclaimed features such as the canal network. As a result of the major re-design of the city centre there is now a clear pedestrian route between New Street Station and Brindley Place, which passes through three of the major squares. This open space network and the city centre strategy provided the framework within which to consider the creation of new small city parks.

City Centre Gardens and St Thomas's Peace Gardens lie within the Greater Convention Centre quarter which has been the focus of much of the redevelopment of the city. They are part of the series of new public spaces - Victoria Square, Centenary Square, the Canalside walks, Churchyards, Peace Gardens and City Centre gardens - that provide the context for local as well as international events. They are part of the plan to support pedestrians throughout the city centre as well as to create a facility for local residents and schools.

St Thomas's Peace Garden

St Thomas's Peace Garden is a small pocket park of approximately 1 acre which contains the remains of the former St Thomas Church built in 1829. The church was damaged during the Second World War and the surrounding graveyard was converted into low key public open space in the 1950s. The scheme was jointly initiated by the Departments of Planning and Architecture and Leisure and Community Services in response to ideas put forward by children from a nearby school. The brief incorporated the children's ideas for a peace park together with the relocation of a colonnaded war memorial which had to be re-sited due to the creation of Centenary Square.

The Landscape Practice Group led a multi-disciplinary design team and liaised closely with the artist Anurhada Patel and with children from Lea Mason School to develop the Peace Garden's concept including designs for the boundary railings and gates. The project also managed to bring together a wide range of people from different religious and cultural backgrounds.

The project cost £600,000 to complete and was funded by Birmingham City Council with financial assistance from the European Regional Development Fund, West Midlands Arts Board and the Junior Chambers of Commerce.

City Centre Gardens

City Centre Gardens is a small neighbourhood park of 1.2 acres which was created on the site of a former council depot and car-park. The gardens became the first park to be laid out in the city centre for decades. The local community were consulted at every stage of the design and development of the park and influenced the decision to build an enclosed park with gates.

The scheme includes a system of pathways with lighting along the main routes; it has detailed decorative boundary railings and gates, a central timber pergola with seating, floodlit tree planting and close mown lawns for sitting on.

A total of £300,000 was spent on the development of the park and it was paid for by the City Council, as part of the infrastructure works of the Broad Street Redevelopment Area.

The city centre parks were part of an integrated approach to the regeneration of the public environment within Birmingham city centre. The Urban Design Study and subsequent studies of specific sites, corridors and quarters provided a comprehensive, co-ordinated and high quality framework for public and private development. This has enabled the city to gain benefits from private developers. Brindley Place has included investment in public infrastructure by the developer with the layout of a new public square within the project. The funding for the two parks was part of the £21 million package of 'City Centre Enhancements'. They were not seen as one-off projects (although residents had to fight hard, in the first instance, for the city centre gardens and resist the proposed private development of a new car-park) but were part of a bigger picture emerging of Birmingham city centre.

The two new parks enhance the character of their quarter and they help to provide a useful facility for the residential population within the city centre. St Thomas's Peace Gardens is the result of collaboration between different cultural and religious groups and serves to represent the multi-racial character of modern Birmingham.

Contacts:

Ann Wood

Landscape Practice Group,

Birmingham City Council, Baskerville House,

Broad Street, Birmingham B1 2NA

Tel: 0121 235 4240

Geoff Wright

City Centre Planning,

Birmingham City Council

Department of Planning and Architecture,

Birmingham City Council, Baskerville House,

Broad Street, Birmingham B1 2NA

Tel: 0121 235 3075

3.17 Urban forestry in parks:
National Urban Forestry Unit

Key themes
- ◆ Partnership funding
- ◆ Community involvement
- ◆ New skills

The Black Country Urban Forestry Unit was set up as an independent organisation in 1990 by the West Midlands region of the Department of the Environment, in partnership with the four Black Country Metropolitan Borough Councils and a number of other agencies from the public, private and voluntary sectors. In 1995, the unit was given a national remit by the DoE to develop, practice and promote the concept of urban forestry. The mission of the National Urban Forestry Unit is to help create a more tree-rich environment as one important means to improving the quality of urban life. The unit wishes to encourage a bolder strategic approach to the development of woodland in towns to provide a national focus for the exchange of information and to increase understanding and popular support for trees in towns.

Urban forestry in parks

As the Black Country Urban Forestry Unit, staff were involved in the 'Urban Forestry in Parks' project set up in partnership with Walsall Metropolitan Borough Council, Leisure Services and the Countryside Commission, which ran in Walsall between 1992 and 1995. The aim of the project was to demonstrate how involving communities in the introduction of natural woodland habitats could aid parks regeneration.

The project included activities such as art projects, landscape history events and demonstrations of woodland management, coppicing and craft skills. The Forestry Unit carried out some work in local schools designed to increase the understanding of woodland ecology and these visits were often carried out in preparation for tree-planting events.

Parks history walks were also an important feature of the urban forestry projects. These looked at the social and industrial history of the community around the park and related this to features in the park landscape. For example, coal pit spoil mounds, and old agricultural features could often be traced in the landscape.

The project also set out to demonstrate the cost effectiveness of amenity woodland management, and to prove that such an approach allows for much greater financial flexibility in the overall management of a park.

Pleck Park

Pleck Park is on the edge of Walsall. The M6 motorway runs along one side of the park on a raised platform and dominates and overwhelms the park. Pleck Park was the site of a community arts project under the umbrella of the Urban Forestry in Parks Project run by the Black Country Urban Forestry Unit in 1993. Bostin Arts were employed on a 3 month contract to generate community interest. The team worked with local groups making sculptures and planting trees.

The motorway was a major intrusion across one side of the park, and apart from the noise and pollution, park-users felt that it destroyed the park's sense of privacy. To counteract this, the Urban Forestry Unit planted 6000 trees in an area of 1.5 hectares along the edge of the park near the motorway.

In its three year life span the Urban Forestry in Parks project involved over 3000 local people, created over 6 hectares (15 acres) of woodland and managed almost 10 hectares (22.5 acres). The work of the project was recognised by the Institute of Leisure and Amenity Management in their Open Space Management Award by gaining a 'Highly Commended' status.

As an independent specialist organisation, the Black Country Urban Forestry Unit was able to broker partnerships between local authorities, community groups and other agencies such as the Countryside Commission.

Contact: Judy Walker,
National Urban Forestry Unit,
Red House, Hill Lane Great Barr,
West Midlands B43 6LZ.
Tel: 0121 358 1414

3.18 Community park:
Bromley-by-Bow Centre

Key themes
◆ Community trust management
◆ Partnership funding
◆ Community development

The regeneration of Bromley-by-Bow, a small area of east London with many problems of social disadvantage, is principally focused on renewing the local park, and work has already begun. Until very recently the park was under-used and in poor condition. However, the Bromley-by-Bow Centre, which abuts the park, is proposing to make the building of a new health centre the trigger for making the park once again a centre of community life. This has been made possible by the transfer of the park's management and maintenance, under agreed terms, from the local authority to the Bromley-by-Bow Centre (a charity), which is able to raise other funds for future development. The park will be the centre of an integrated development, linking the arts, enterprise, health and community care, and will be the first initiative of its kind, as far as is known, in the UK.

The Bromley-by-Bow Centre submitted a bid for SRB money in partnership with Stratford Development Partnerships Ltd, with the support of the local authority and many private sector businesses. The total programme is expected to lever in £4 million, of which £2 million will come from the private sector. The Bromley-by-Bow Centre is a charitable trust, community owned but professionally managed, and has a long track record of successful community development. The refurbishment and renewal of the park (still known locally as 'Bob's Park' after the park-keeper who looked after it until he retired some years ago) is the Centre's biggest challenge yet.

Contact: Andrew Mawson,
Bromley-by-Bow Centre, 1 Bruce Road,
Bromley-by-Bow, London E3 3HN
Tel: 0181 980 4618

3.19 Parks initiatives:
Calderdale Council

Shibden Park, Halifax

Key themes

◆ Income generation

◆ Site management group

◆ Providing an infrastructure of car-parking, toilets and refreshments

Shibden Park is a park of 32 hectares in Halifax, and the site of Shibden Hall, now a folk museum. It is an urban park that in recent years has been developed to make it a regional attraction, particularly for families.

Cars are allowed to drive into the park a short way, before entering a free car-park. From there the many visitors have a fine landscaped park to walk through, an opportunity to visit the museum, but there are also many other attractions which have been developed in partnership with local commercial operators on a franchise basis, including:

◆ Tractor train which offers rides through the park;

◆ Boating lake;

◆ Pitch and putt;

◆ Kiosk and café;

◆ Children's rides;

◆ Grass sledges;

◆ Miniature railway.

In addition there are the usual free attractions of a children's playground, paddling pool, ornamental pond, orienteering games and football pitches, backed up by fully accessible toilets.

Although it is clearly a local authority park, there is also a park management group involving the franchisees and a local tourism officer, who work together to promote the park. Attendances of up to 15,000 visitors on a single Sunday were recorded in the summer of 1995. Income generated by the franchises makes a substantial contribution to the high quality maintenance of the park.

Wellholme Park, Brighouse

Key themes

◆ Community involvement

◆ Income generation

◆ Disability access

Wellholme Park is one of 19 parks in Calderdale where games facilities are now managed by a local community group under the Council's self-management programme. The majority of these sites have bowling greens where bowling clubs were often the focus for developing greater community involvement in the management of the parks, even though their remit now extends to running facilities such as tennis courts, playgrounds, and pitch and putt greens.

In general the scheme has been a great success, and Wellholme Park is certainly an example of high standards of management and a wider provision of facilities achieved through local community pride.

Wellholme Park is 14.6 hectares, and offers:

◆ Woodland;

◆ Open green space;

◆ Football and rugby pitches;

◆ Two crown bowling greens;

◆ Flat bowling green for a visually impaired bowling club;

◆ Four tennis courts;

◆ Crazy golf course and swingball;

◆ Club house with residential; accommodation.

The council have made a significant investment in the new tennis courts and the bowling greens, but have been happy to do this because of the high level of care and management subsequently provided by the Woodvale Bowling Club which co-ordinates community involvement.

All fees collected from the use of the bowling greens, tennis courts and crazy golf, are kept by the club and used to re-invest in new

facilities, for example, the flat bowling green for use by the Pennine Bowling Club for the Visually Handicapped. Volunteers staff a ticket office to collect fees.

In general, park self-management groups charge lower rates than Calderdale's recommended prices and offer a wide variety of concessionary rates. All community groups operate within the council's Equal Opportunities Policy.

Poop Scoop Bylaws in Calderdale

Key themes

◆ A solution was found to the dog-fouling problem

In response to growing public concern at dog-fouling in parks, Calderdale Council sought to secure agreement from the DoE to operate 'poop scoop bylaws' in 12 of its parks and 6 of its children's playgrounds. Several years of voluntary schemes had failed to make any inroads into the problem.

Securing bylaws is a lengthy and expensive business, and requires a serious commitment by the local authority to enforce them. In October 1994 government agreement to the bylaws was enacted, after the council had proven that it had the financial resources to provide adequate dog litter bins in the 12 parks and 6 playgrounds, to empty them regularly, and to be able to provide the staffing necessary to enforce the bylaws. A fine of £500 was imposed on any person who allows their dog to foul one of the designated spaces, and a big publicity campaign was organised to announce the arrival of the bylaws - and the draconian fines. The results were immediate, with a sudden cessation of dog fouling. So far there have been no prosecutions.

The greatest drawback to the scheme is the very high revenue costs of operating and maintaining dog litter bins to the standards required by the bylaw, possibly as much as is spent on grounds maintenance for each park.

Contact: Bob Kaye,
Senior Development Officer, Calderdale Council Leisure Services,
Wellesley Park, Halifax HX2 0AY
Tel: 01422 359454

3.20 Monitoring parks costs:
Victoria Park, Cardiff

Key themes

◆ Monitoring
◆ Value for money

In co-operation with Cardiff City Council Leisure and Amenities Department, a study was undertaken to examine and attribute all costs associated with the management and maintenance of just one park in its service, Victoria Park in the west of the city. In addition surveys were undertaken to estimate how many visits were made each year. With these two sets of information, it became possible to broadly estimate the cost per visit, and thus put the funding of parks on the same kind of value for money footing as other forms of leisure provision.

Victoria Park, Cardiff was established between 1894 and 1897 from a section of Ely Common. It occupies 20 acres of ground, and is in many ways a typical Victorian town park with ornamental flower beds and mature trees, and railings on all sides.

Facilities include:

◆ A paddling pool;
◆ A children's play area ;
◆ Tennis courts;
◆ Bowling green;
◆ Bowling pavilion (also hired out for nursery use);
◆ Toilet block.

The immediate area is predominantly a white middle-class suburb, with a small ethnic minority population, but with some rented housing to the south. As such it provides the social mix that is often almost a guarantee of park success.

Numbers of visits

Surveys of numbers of people entering the park were carried out in early autumn, and unfortunately in bad weather. It was clear that most users were 'committed' users - dog walkers, adults taking children to play on the swings, taking a short cut, teenagers hanging out - rather than opportunistic users taking advantage of fine weather to use the paddling pool or play games. Yet with approximately 1,000 visitors recorded on both survey days, it was reasonable to assume that Victoria Park received on average 1,000 visits a day throughout the year. (Given that the researchers did not count official uses such as school sports days, community events, higher use of sports facilities in good weather, the figure is likely to be on the conservative side). From these figures one would extrapolate an annual number of visits of 350,000, in what is certainly not one of the busiest parks in the city, indicating just how well-used parks can be.

Costs of providing the park

Costs of providing the park in terms of annual revenue costs plus an element of capital expenditure taken from an average spend over 5 years were itemised. For contractual reasons these figures are commercially sensitive, and therefore confidential, but were based on the following categories:

Costs

◆ Grounds maintenance;

◆ Provision items;

◆ Variation Orders;

◆ Ranger Service staff costs;

◆ Maintenance of pool plant;

◆ Repair and maintenance of building and facilities;

◆ Water, electricity and phone charges;

◆ Insurance;

◆ Staff/management contract costs for supervising bowls pavilion, pool hut, tennis courts and toilets;

◆ Client costs of managing contract.

Income

◆ Bowling green, tennis courts, deck chairs;

◆ Rent from nursery;

◆ Income from an ice cream van licence.

Cost per visit

The overall cost of managing and maintaining Victoria Park based on figures taken from 1993/1994 accounts, was approximately £181,000. Even using the low figure of 350,000 visits per annum, this would work out at a subsidy level of no more than 50p per visit, probably less. Many people would regard this as a 'value for money' investment in urban recreational provision, particularly because of the wide range of people who use parks (some of whom, like the elderly or the poor who may not use any other form of leisure provision, public or private), and that those who use them do so regularly, mostly walk to them, and therefore exact no great environmental cost in terms of car use.

In these terms the annual revenue cost of Victoria Park is really quite small, and the 'subsidised' cost per visit of 50p, can be compared favourably to the average cost per visit of a public library of about £1.30, or of a swim in a public pool of over £2 per swim. The park holds its own therefore, in a portfolio of public leisure provision that cannot be wholly provided without subsidy, and as a central part of the range of public leisure facilities that enhance the quality of community life for many people, particularly those with a low level of disposable income, but who welcome the opportunity to go out regularly. This kind of detailed measurement of costs set against use, while not applicable to many kinds of urban open space, is valuable for those kinds of urban parks which are primarily provided for active recreational use by all members of the family or community.

Contact: John Scrimgeour,
Leisure & Amenities, City of Cardiff,
Heath Park, Cardiff CF4 4EP
Tel: 01222 751235

3.21 Castlefield Urban Heritage Park, Manchester

Key themes

◆ Urban regeneration

◆ Tourism

◆ Management company

◆ Partnership funding

◆ New skills

The Castlefield area of Manchester is something of an enigma, as it serves as an excellent case-study of innovative development which does not fit readily into familiar definitions of public parks. It could equally, however, be cited as a model of urban regeneration as a 'quarter' of a city.

A major tourist attraction

Castlefield is now one of the major tourism destinations in the north of England, attracting approximately one million visitors per year. At the same time the area is home to businesses which do not see themselves as part of the tourism or leisure industry. Time will tell whether this sharing of Castlefield's resources between tourism, education and commerce is sustainable; but the early indications would suggest that it is, in fact, the key to sustainability. Castlefield is a working part of the city of Manchester, not a hollow theme park.

A period of decline in Castlefield had mirrored that of many other parts of Manchester's fabric, with low grade activities moving in to exploit the cheap land values and rents after the original economic activities ceased.

A partnership success

Metamorphosis from 'twilight zone' to Heritage Park has been engineered by an uncommonly sustained planning strategy, in which Manchester City Council, the former Greater Manchester County Council and the Central Manchester Development Corporation have all been highly proactive, with political and financial encouragement from the DoE. As the frustration of slow,

early progress has given way to the euphoria of success, all these agents now compete for the credit but the truth is that no one of them could have achieved it all without the others and without some visionary investments by the private sector.

The private sector is now buoyant in Castlefield, but the initial confidence was demonstrated by a select few, most notably bookmaker Jim Ramsbottom. Granada Television have also acted as a potent generator, with the development of their Studio Tours. These early 'toes in the water' made it easier to encourage other key names such as YMCA and YHA to invest in flagship developments which add to the leisure and tourism profile.

A seamless network

Visitors to Castlefield are provided with information by an assortment of means, the centrepiece being the Visitor Centre on Liverpool Road. Abundant signage is provided throughout the area and numerous interpretative boards provide written and graphic information about specific locations and artifacts. In addition there is a unique urban ranger service, with uniformed rangers to help and guide visitors.

Castlefield Management Company

The Visitor Centre, Ranger Service and other management services are the responsibility of the Castlefield Management Company, which is a 'not-for-profit' limited company set up through partnership between the public and private sectors in the area. Inspired by a similar model in Lowell, USA, the management company was advocated by leisure consultants L&R, who were appointed to advise on the best way to take forward Castlefield's long term management and maintenance needs. These needs had previously been identified as part of a broader ranging English Tourist Board Strategic Development Initiative (SDI) for Manchester, Salford and Trafford.

The Management Company is a very important facet of Castlefield's distinctiveness and is probably as vital to the sustainability of the heritage park concept as the spirit of partnership in developing the fabric of the park. The company's existence ensures that the area's identity will always be defended and there will be someone striving to generate funds for upkeep and ongoing investment. At present the company exists in the form of a pilot management initiative, for a prospective term of three years, with the following key operators and landowners represented on a Steering Group:

Manchester City Council

Salford City Council

Museum of Science and Industry

Granada Studio Tour

Manchester Ship Canal Company

Specimen Properties

North West Tourist Board.

The declared objectives of the pilot initiative include:

◆ The provision a team of 'Urban Rangers' trained to assist the operators, landowners and visitors to the Castlefield area;

◆ Establishing good working relations with the operators and landowners in Castlefield;

◆ Increasing the number of staying and day visitors to the area;

◆ Expanding and improving the existing system of signing, orientation and interpretation for visitors;

◆ Establishing the permanent Management Company.

The twentieth century appears to have offered the area little new in the form of street furniture. A new footbridge emerged from a design competition but, on the whole, bollards seats and lighting lay undue emphasis on the Victorian flavour. Castlefield is designated as both Urban Heritage Park and Conservation Area. Conservation Area status often stifles imaginative and contemporary design. When so many ages are being represented here perhaps more liberty should be granted to contemporary designers to produce a showcase and celebrate the concept of a park.

Castlefield does not have conspicuous edges or boundaries, although there are rather unobtrusive signs on the major roads as they enter the area and many of the structures are recognisable landmarks. In one sense this gives the lie to its designation as a park but its ability to survive in the long term may be at least as dependent upon a more diverse economic role as an integrated increment of the city.

Contact: Castlefield Management Company, The Castlefield Centre, 101 Liverpool Road, Castlefield, Manchester M3 4JN

Tel: 0161 834 4026

3.22 Centre of the Earth, Birmingham

Key theme

◆ Environmental education

The Centre of the Earth is an environmental education centre situated on a one hectare site about one mile from the centre of Birmingham, established 5 years ago and owned and managed by the Urban Wildlife Trust. The land it now occupies was abandoned and the site was developed to attract wildlife and to stimulate children's awareness of the environment. The centre itself was purpose-built using environmentally friendly technology and designed by architect David Leigh. The Centre's grounds were landscaped with sustainability in mind, and a range of re-cycled and reclaimed materials have been incorporated in the design.

It receives some funding from Birmingham City Council's Department of Environment and Department of Leisure and Community Services, as well as support from other private sector and charitable sources.

Primarily focusing on schools to deliver environmental educational activities, the centre offers projects based on five themes:

◆ Art and environment;

◆ Making local-global links by drawing attention to the relationship between everyday items and their implications for the environment;

◆ Earth education which uses a sensory approach to discovering the natural environment and introduces broad concepts such as food webs;

◆ Urban ecology and bio-diversity;

◆ Looking at the environmental impact of energy production and how to minimise this.

The centre employs two permanent workers - the Co-ordinator, Graham Peake and the Education Officer, Andrew Simons. Otherwise, it relies on volunteers, placements or sessional workers. Consequently out of school hours activity is limited, although it supports a playgroup and a youth group for 11-19 year olds.

During summer months, 5 day residential trips under the banner 'Sunship Earth' are organised to the Wyre Forest in Worcestershire for 8-12 year olds. One popular activity is Mr Sun's Restaurant where children sit around a table in the forest to discuss the food chain and energy. The ratio of adults to children on these trips is quite high at 1 to 3.

The one hectare site has been designed to give the impression of a larger scale. It is contoured, supports two dipping ponds, a bog, woodland glades and circular open areas. This ensures privacy for different groups using the site simultaneously.

More informally, it is used by children after school as a meeting place and play area. Children prefer to play in the centre's grounds rather than the adjacent playground with equipment which is poorly designed with a concrete base. Staff are on duty at the centre until 5pm each weekday except Wednesdays when it remains open until 8pm offering parents and guardians a sense of security for their children. Older children and young adults sometimes 'hang out' after hours but no real damage has been sustained by the centre or the grounds.

Consolidating the environmental education programme for schools is seen as a priority in ensuring the centre's future financial liability. It is proposed that a youth worker be employed to develop the youth programme. Graham Peake also sees the

Centre as a resource for groups and individuals discussing Agenda 21 issues.

Contact: Graham Peake, Co-ordinator, Centre of the Earth, 42 Norman Street, Winson Green, Birmingham B18 7EP

Tel: 0121 5151702

3.23 Parks and the DSO:

Cheltenham Borough Council

Key theme

◆ CCT contracts

Cheltenham Borough Council has shown how a DSO can compete with the private sector and win, while still ensuring the highest standards in parks maintenance. The Landscape Services Division of Cheltenham's Operational Services DSO handles maintenance of the council's own parks, but has also twice won the contract for those in Stratford-upon-Avon, worth some £300,000 a year. It also has contracts with Gloucestershire County Council, the District Health Authority, several parish councils and a number of clients.

The success of the DSO's working relationship with its clients lies in a clear division of responsibility, and close day-to-day contact. By emphasising reliability, and operating openly and honestly, the DSO staff have built trust between themselves and their clients. Weekly management meetings help ensure that things are dealt with before they become problems. This has not been achieved through formal quality control mechanisms like BS5750, but through developing the DSO's own approach to quality in management through teamwork. The fact that Cheltenham and Stratford-upon-Avon won their respective classes in the 1995 Britain in Bloom competition offers an external measure of the quality achieved by the DSO.

The DSO is now keen to extend its work to cover all aspects of parks management, not just maintenance, believing not only that it has the skills to do so, but that there is much it could do to enhance the parks it maintains, if it had a freer hand.

Contact: John Rees, Landscape Services Manager, Operational Services Department, Cheltenham Borough Council, Central Depot, Swindon Road, Cheltenham, Gloucestershire GL51 9JZ
Tel: 01242 232594 x 2555

3.24 One o'clock clubs and events in parks:

London Borough of Lambeth

Key themes

◆ Children's play

◆ Community involvement

One O'Clock clubs in parks

The London Borough of Lambeth run 14 one o'clock clubs for under-5s, all of which are located in parks. The clubs are open most weekday afternoons. Lambeth made a deliberate policy decision to place one o'clock clubs in the parks as part of their overall management approach. By their presence, the clubs help to create a sense of safety as well as encouraging social contact between local parents, that may otherwise be difficult in an inner-city area. The clubs are well-supported and well-used by local families. Park managers say that some of their most effective consultative surveys are carried out through the one o'clock clubs, where people are prepared to take part and express considered views.

The presence of a well supported one o'clock club in a park helps to create a positive sense of management of the park as well as providing a focal point for people with young children in the surrounding area. In the winter months, when it gets dark early, the bright lights and busy-ness of the club buildings create a sense of safety and activity to other park-users.

The council also runs 10 staffed adventure playgrounds, many of them in parks, and grant-aids others, as part of its commitment to children's play. These are open in school term times from 3.30 - 8.30pm and during school holidays from 10am to 6pm.

The provision of staffed play facilities in parks has been given as a reason for the surprisingly low level of vandalism and graffiti in Lambeth parks, particularly when compared to the levels of graffiti in neighbouring streets. It is suggested that the loyalty and esteem engendered by Lambeth's commitment to play in parks may partially account for this.

Events in parks

Lambeth Parks Services is also strongly committed to events in parks. There is a wide programme of both council organised and community organised events, including the Mela (Asian Festival) on Streatham Common and Country Show in Brockwell Park (which attracts nearly 150,000 visitors over two days). Community events have included the annual Gay Pride, held for many years in Brockwell Park, and Reggae Sunsplash, Gran Gran Fiesta, National Music Day and many small events on Clapham Common. Events help to create a positive feel to a park and as Lambeth officers suggest, many people who may not use the park on their own, feel more secure and more welcome in the park when an event is taking place. Small events are seen as particularly important to help to establish use of local parks. Small parks can be used as venues for all sorts of local groups who wish to promote their own activities. Most smaller events take place free of charge, however the larger events can provide a source of income as Lambeth now charges for commercial and fund-raising events.

Contact: Jeanne McNair, Lambeth Parks Services, 5th Floor, Courtney House, 9 - 15 New Park Road, Brixton Hill, London SW2
Tel: 0171 926 0139

3.25 Cannon Hill Park,

Birmingham

Key themes

◆ Buildings in parks

◆ Events

◆ Providing an infrastructure of parking, toilets and refreshments

Buildings in parks

The Midlands Arts Centre and the Cannon Hill Nature Centre are both based in Cannon Hill Park. Built facilities in the park present both problems and opportunities. They attract people to the park and provide important facilities which support people's use of the park, such as café and toilets. In turn, the park attracts people who gradually get to know and use the Arts Centre. The drawbacks to the presence of buildings in the park revolve around questions of security, particularly after dark, when the Arts Centre is open but the park is 'closed' although not locked.

Cannon Hill Park

Cannon Hill park is a large park of 240 acres. It is situated about two miles from Birmingham city centre and receives one million visits a year. The park has a large expanse of conservation land, 80 acres of formal park land, a lake, sports grounds and formal gardens. The park is open every day from 7.30am to dusk.

Cannon Hill Park has a good reputation for horticulture and leisure features such as a boating lake, canoe pool, putting and bowling greens, and a children's play area. The park is used for a large number of events which are mostly free. The authority estimates that there are 1 million visits made to the park every year.

Midlands Arts Centre

The Midlands Arts Centre (MAC) is open 15 hours a day, 362 days a year. It is an important and established arts venue and a centre for arts courses/classes. The Arts Centre staff have in recent years opened up

the centre to the park. As well as building a terraced area, opening up the café and bar to the park, they have begun to develop small pieces of external art work. The Centre has its own outdoor theatre and runs a regular summer programme of weekend concerts; it has recently organised some prestigious events in the park. The Arts Centre café and bar is a popular place for weekend family outings, it is one of the few social places that can cater for family visits.

The Nature Centre

The Nature Centre occupies six and half acres, and houses 134 species of wildlife which are kept in surroundings as similar as possible to their natural habitats. Otters, beavers and fish can be observed from special underwater windows. It has a picnic area and a café and between March and October it is open between 10am and 5pm.

From April to December 1995, the Nature Centre received 107,468 visits. Visits are free for children up to 15.

Advantages and disadvantages of built facilities in the park

These facilities together make up a significant arts, leisure and educational attraction for south Birmingham. Although they are not managed as a single entity, a Consultative Committee, which includes the park, arts centre and nature centre, meet regularly to plan future activities and to organise the publicity of events. The benefits of having the arts centre located in the park were summed up as follows:

◆ By offering a number of activities for children and schools, the arts centre attracts both children and families who might otherwise not have visited the park. Similarly, MAC is accessible to people visiting the park but may not otherwise have visited an arts centre;

◆ Programming of events by the park events team and MAC can be complementary, especially events, play schemes and classes for children;

◆ The presence of the arts centre is useful as a focal point in the park, it provides a place to meet, café, bar and toilets;

The arts centre, the nature centre and the park staff have a working relationship; they plan events together, and meet on a regular basis.

Security has been a problem in recent years. Until eight years ago the Arts Centre was a membership organisation and people had to show their card before entering. Now the centre is much more freely accessible and more open to the risk of crime and vandalism, particularly after dark. Although the park is in theory closed and therefore unstaffed, it is not locked or secure. For people walking to the arts centre in the evening, the dark can be unsettling.

The possible drawbacks to the siting of the arts centre in the park are:

◆ The arts centre is open in the evenings while the park is closed. This can pose problems for security, particularly around the car park where most of the vandalism problems occur.

◆ On the occasions of large events in the park, demand on the arts centre building can be overwhelming.

◆ Current joint planning arrangements between arts centre and park management are not always adequate and will need to be strengthened to support long-term plans.

Contact: John Greenhouse,
Cannon Hill Park, Information Centre,
Cannon Hill Park, Moseley,
Birmingham B12 9QH
Tel: 0121 4490238
Geoff Simms,
Midlands Arts Centre
Tel: 0121 4404221

3.26 Visual Arts Co-ordinator for outdoor arts:

London Borough of Merton

Key themes
◆ Public art
◆ Community involvement
◆ New skills

In 1990, the London Borough of Merton, Greater London Arts and Wimbledon School of Art collaborated to establish a temporary post of Visual Arts Co-ordinator. The work was mainly concerned with landscaping and sculpture projects with schools and in local parks in the London Borough of Merton. The arts co-ordinator set up many projects involving artists with local schools, youth and local residents groups. The immediate success led to the development of a particular theme - 'artists on playgrounds'. In turn, this has led to an emphasis on outdoor arts projects, almost a 'green arts approach' where artworks in playgrounds and parks (including tree planting, water features, and sculptural seating) have complimented the wider strategic management of public open space. The post illustrates the creative potential for projects that involve new skills, such as those of artists, in parks.

The co-ordinator has organised projects improving 20 school grounds and several projects in parks such as seating, arrangement of bedding plants, the creation of gateways and entrances and other temporary events. All the projects she has run involve collaboration between artists, children and residents. Most of the projects were overseen and planned in detail by a local group. The post has highlighted the potential for outdoor arts projects, which have environmental, educational and play features.

◆ The environmental art projects were also part of Merton's Playground Group which brought together the borough's arts, arboricultural, technical, environmental and education officers to devise a detailed and soundly based outdoor play policy for the borough.

- The link between arts and ecology was also made in tree dressing festivals, in local parks and in projects such as the generation of power from a water wheel in a local river.

- The London Arts Board funded a collaboration between artists and local youth clubs to run outdoor events.

Contact: Robert Hobbs,

Assistant Director of Leisure,

London Borough of Merton, Crown House,

London Road, Morden, Surrey SM4 5DX

Tel: 0181 545 3651

3.27 Playgroups and nursery schools in parks:

Mid-Sussex District Council

Key themes
- Buildings in parks
- Children's play

Parks are a good place to locate children's nursery or playgroup provision, where they are surrounded by grass and trees, rather than streets and cars. In Mid-Sussex the policy is to integrate indoor and outdoor leisure provision, and bring them both up to the same standards of quality, and this has created new opportunities for children's early learning as well as making a welcome addition to income generation in such a service.

The King's Centre at East Grinstead, located in 12 acres of park land, is a leisure centre opened in April 1995 and built on what had been a typical, run down recreation ground in the middle of the town. The new centre contains a swimming pool, sports hall, fitness centre, dedicated creche and sauna, together with a room designed for play-groups, and changing rooms for people using the outdoor sports pitches. It has a café-restaurant with views out on to the park.

The leisure centre provides a base for managing the site, and an adjacent park, Mount Noddy. There is a natural lake in the park, well fenced off, used by local young

people who join an informal angling club, programmed from the centre. There is a well-designed toddler's playground, immediately adjacent to the playgroup room in the centre, which the playgroup children use most days in good weather, but it is also a public facility.

The teams who pay to use the pitches, and have the use of high quality changing rooms with shower facilities, also have the use of the café-restaurant and bar. There is a local GP referral scheme, encouraging patients to use the leisure centre, and therefore the park.

Mount Noddy, also in East Grinstead, is a traditional landscaped park from Victorian times, with separate putting green, bowling green, children's playground, football pitch, ornamental flowerbeds, and general grassed areas. There are floodlit multi-purpose sports courts, a new park centre/pavilion and car parking for 33 vehicles. The park was in a very run-down state until about seven years ago when the council decided to take action to remedy the decline. A significant sum of money has been spent on new features such as the large pavilion right in the centre of the park, which accommodates changing rooms and club room for the bowls club, a refreshment kiosk, and community rooms available for nursery use during the day. A Montessori group hires the pavilion for a play group which is held every week day.

As with many sites, there were a few problems with vandalism at one time: new saplings were uprooted or broken, and there was damage to buildings. The council's policy is to repair such damage where possible within 24 hours through monitoring the sites regularly, thereby keeping the problem under control. Over time vandalism has decreased as a result of this policy. The kiosk within the centre is open at weekends and most days during the summer months.

Lessons from Mid-Sussex

In both cases, what had been under-used and rather time-worn public spaces have been revived and given a new life by the investment in new leisure buildings offering appropriate facilities for activities and refreshment. Together with the provision of car parking, this has made them much busier - and safer - places. The demand for under-five's provision has also provided revenue for the local authority in the form of rents and hiring fees for premises, while creating an ideal setting for local pre-school provision.

In summary the case-study shows the value of:

◆ The integration of indoor and outdoor leisure;

◆ On-site management and a ranger service;

◆ New buildings and facilities.

Contact: Ian Burton,

Mid-Sussex District Council, Oaklands,

Oaklands Road, Haywards Heath,

West Sussex RH16 1SS

Tel: 01444 458166

3.28 Play strategy:
North Hertfordshire District Council

Key themes

◆ Parks strategy

◆ Consultation

◆ Disability access

◆ Children's play

In 1991 North Herts District Council undertook a survey of all the play areas provided by the council, and found many of them to be seriously out-dated, the equipment worn out and often missing. A comprehensive policy was therefore decided upon, partly based on the National Playing Fields Association (NPFA) standards of provision, but also on assessing local need and demand through consultation with local parents. Particular reference was made to the needs of children with disabilities.

The most common form of provision was a play area for younger children, with the addition of plentiful seating for adults close to the play area, as well as picnic tables and benches to encourage family use. The reason for lower levels of vandalism in the play areas is thought to be greater popularity and use.

Provision for teenagers was also regarded as important, although this still largely takes the form of provision for informal games of football and basketball, dominated by young males. However, areas with robust equipment designed for the needs of teenagers are proving very popular with both sexes. A strong visual distinction is made between teenagers and young children's areas by the use of different colours and materials, and this also appears to work well.

Great importance is also attached to ensuring that play areas offer integrated play opportunities for children with disabilities and special needs, and equipment specifically designed for integrated play has been sought out and used.

The authority has attempted to 'design-in' problem behaviour (such as riding on pathways shared with elderly people), by developing local cycle tracks, and providing simulated roadways for younger children designed to encourage greater road safety consciousness.

Contact: J.Tuck,

Parks and Open Space Officer,

North Herts District Council, Gernon Road,

Letchworth, Herts SG6 3JF

Tel: 01462 474272

3.29 Parks and open spaces strategy & parks community development officer:
London Borough of Newham

Key themes

◆ Parks strategy

◆ Community development

Parks and open spaces strategy

The London Borough of Newham has agreed a draft strategy for their parks and open spaces, prepared by consultant, Alan Barber, and currently (early 1996) subject to public consultation. The draft strategy is built around four main themes that are relevant to the borough as a whole, hence the draft strategy

integrates the parks service with key corporate concerns. These themes are:

Parks and the active citizen

Sets out ways to make parks a central part of the Borough's plans for community development.

Parks and the urban landscape

To set parks and open spaces within a borough-wide Landscape Strategy.

Parks and sustainable environment

To incorporate parks within the environmental programme to be developed as part of Agenda 21, particularly in developing environmental education which is included within the job descriptions for the Parks Ranger Service.

Parks and the management role

The strategy places great emphasis on park management and its role within Leisure Services.

To pull these broad themes together, the strategy recommends the formation of a Parks Management Team which sees park programming as its main role. The strategy envisages the main responsibilities of a Park Management Team as:

◆ Taking a co-ordinated approach to service provision;

◆ Directing a structured approach to strategy implementation;

◆ Setting and monitoring of service standards;

◆ Reviewing innovations from elsewhere;

◆ Analysing the results of consumer research/market survey;

◆ Carrying out a systematic audit of management procedures for compliance and effectiveness;

◆ Reviewing compliance with departmental action plans;

◆ Producing annual reports of Newham park services.

Newham Community Parks Development Officer

The London Borough of Newham has a community parks development officer based in Newham's parks client services unit. The post was created in 1993, to: create greater awareness of all aspects of the Parks Service, particularly in relation to environmental/ecological issues and to maximise usage and community participation. The role of the development officer is to organise a regular series of events and activities in the borough's parks working with community groups, schools, community centres, the library service, the city farm, sports and recreation staff and the summer play schemes.

The officer carries out research on park use, including surveys and discussion groups. In her first year in post, she was very involved in the establishment of a new park built on the site of an old maternity hospital. Her role was to contact community groups and residents and to facilitate ways in which they could become involved in the design, development and subsequent use of the park. She helped to establish a play group and set up an After Schools Club based in the park. A summer play scheme was introduced and a number of community groups now use the new pavilion for regular meetings and events. Her role was pivotal to the careful development of the new park. She is also a key figure in facilitating park use for groups such as the elderly, mothers and toddler groups, schools and others. For example, she has worked with local disabled groups to improve disabled access to parks and she organises trips to the park from local day-care centres.

In many ways the community development worker has paved the way for the introduction of the Newham parks ranger service. She has established a network of groups and organisations whom the park rangers can contact to discuss events, activities and other developments in the parks.

Contact: Peter Appleton, Manager, Parks Client Services Unit, Leisure Services,

London Borough of Newham,

Balaam Street, Park, Greengate Street, Plaistow, London E13 OAS

Tel: 0181 472 1430

3.30 DSO and parks maintenance:

Oldham MBC

Key theme

◆ CCT contracts

In Oldham, the parks maintenance contract was won by the Council's DSO, and the partnership between client and contractor is a good example of how, effectively applied, CCT has brought clarity to parks management and improvements in service to the public.

The client-side managers believe that working with the Council's DSO offers greater value because it is much easier to re-negotiate aspects of the contract where the need to make profits is not so acute: for example, it was possible to reach agreement that savings made on grass-cutting during the dry summer of 1995 would be re-allocated to winter maintenance works.

The success of the partnership arises partly from the fact that the DSO secured quality assurance to BS5750 in 1991. From the client side, this guarantees an acceptable standard of work, enabling them to be less concerned about daily routine. Instead they have been able to step back and give more attention to management and development issues. Management staff have been able to devote more of their time to working with the public.

An obvious example of the benefit this has brought is the revival of a local festival, Tulip Sunday. This took place each year in Alexandra Park, but interest and attendances had been falling for some years. It is now held in a different park each year, and acts as a spur for interest and action in each site. A small refurbishment budget ('Tulip Money') is attached to it, and there is fierce competition for the event, which now attracts up to 4,000 people.

The response from the public is that the parks are starting to look better than they have for a long time. Oldham has made progress in establishing Friends of the Park groups, linking schools, local people and ward councillors, and the intention is that these will be serviced by client-side mangers responsible for the relevant contracts. Oldham Council has also established a Forum for Agenda 21 (led by Environmental Services) which has helped to raise the profile of community involvement in parks.

This study highlights

◆ The introduction of BS5750 to guarantee day-by-day standards.

◆ Close involvement of elected members and the public in parks development.

◆ Service improvements, supported by a Borough-wide strategy, concentrating resources to create a tangible impact.

Contact: Steve Smith,

Parks & Countryside Manager, Leisure Services,

Oldham Metropolitan Borough Council, Civic Centre, West Street, Oldham OL1 1UJ

Tel: 0161 911 4642

3.31 Community garden project:

Quaking Houses, Durham

Key themes

◆ Partnership funding
◆ Community involvement

Quaking Houses is a small village in Durham, in which until recently coal-mining was a principal source of employment. Local residents have become engaged in a number of projects to improve the local quality of life, and boost morale in a village which has seen severe problems associated with high unemployment and few local facilities.

The Quaking Houses Youth Club, with the energetic support of a local youth worker Diane Richardson, has successfully completed a community garden for the benefit of all village residents. The project took 14 months to complete, and was funded through a series of partnerships including the following grants:

European Rural Development Fund	£10,540
Barclays Innervision	£2,500

Civic Trust	£2,000
Countryside Commission	£1,690
Durham County Council	£1,750
Derwentside District Council	£1,750

The project organisers adopted a multi-agency approach working alongside Quaking Houses Environmental Trust, West Durham Groundwork Trust, Durham Rural Community Council, Durham County Council and Derwentside District Council.

The finished community garden includes safe play equipment, bench seating, sensory garden, butterfly garden and raised flower beds, and thus has been designed with all sections of the community in mind. The project - which during completion involved more than 150 local people - has helped create a greater degree of understanding between younger and older members of the village, and was one of five prize-winners (from an entry of 522) in the Shell 'Best of Britain' awards for 1995.

This project is one of a number of local initiatives designed to give people greater self-confidence in their ability to improve their local surroundings, even in the midst of difficult local economic and social circumstances.

Contact: Kate Glendinning, Groundwork West Durham, 47-48 Market Place, Bishop Auckland, Co. Durham DL14 7NP Tel: 01388 662666

3.32 Health and fitness development officer:

Birmingham City Council

Key themes
◆ New Skills
◆ Health
◆ Links between indoor and outdoor leisure

The health and fitness development officer's brief is to develop health and fitness projects within Leisure Services. The post was first established in the sports side of Leisure Services but has since broadened; the post holder now integrates questions of health and fitness within the Department of Leisure and Community Services as a whole.

The work includes highlighting health issues within the contracts and the standards established for leisure centres and other facilities. For example, contracts include health and fitness qualifications in staff employment specifications. Café franchise specifications also require healthy foods to be included on menus.

The officer has also made important links with the health authorities who have made funds available for projects in primary health care. The City Council and the Family Health Services, for example, are piloting an 'exercise on prescription' scheme. To manage the scheme, four health and fitness advisors were established in Leisure Centres in four areas of the city. A doctor who decides to prescribe a patient exercise, refers the patient to a health and fitness officer. The officer then spends an hour with the patient carrying out a full fitness appraisal and together they work out a programme of exercise. Many patients wish to start by walking. Basic speeds and pace can be tried out on the treadmill in the gym and then the patient can go out on walks with the parks rangers. However, the rangers' walking programme is geared towards nature watching rather than health. The fitness development officer is keen to establish marked out routes which people can use to follow up their sessions on the treadmills. Exercise on prescription can have a wider remit than the facilities offered within the leisure centre and can encourage people to take up walking and cycling in parks.

Walking has developed as a particular theme for Birmingham's health and fitness officer and it is likely to become important to the work of park rangers. A conference organised by the officer earlier this year, under the banner 'Walking for Healthy Living', brought together planners and health experts and people with an interest in transport and cycling. The conference also promoted a 2 kilometre walking programme developed by a Finnish Institute for Health Promotion. The conference covered issues about safety, attractiveness of the walking environment as well as the constantly publicised concern about levels of health and fitness of people in Britain.

Contact: Ms Ray Davies,

Birmingham City Council, Department of Leisure & Community Services,

PO Box 2122, Baskerville House,

Broad Street, Birmingham B1 2NE

Tel: 0121 235 9944

3.33 Nature conservation and BTCV:

London Borough of Richmond

Key theme

◆ CCT contracts

Most larger councils have had to split up their work into manageable contracts, and this has often been done simply according to location. In the London Borough of Richmond, the split was along specialisms, creating contracts for amenity sites, arboriculture, schools, parks, playgrounds, and nature conservation. The last included woodland sites, riverbanks, as well as major areas like Barnes Common and Ham Lands (a refilled quarry developing as scrub and woodland with hay meadows).

Working with the London Ecology Unit and the London Wildlife Trust, Richmond's parks managers began working out what they wanted to do with this land, much of which had received little or no attention in the past. They invited interest from specialist companies with nature conservation experience and further investigated a dozen potential companies to identify six whose approach coincided with the council's. Five of these submitted tenders.

In January 1994 the contract was won, on price, by BTCV Enterprises Ltd, the commercial arm of the charitable British Trust for Conservation Volunteers. BTCV Enterprises manages the work, which is sub-contracted to about 20 skilled workers, as needs and seasons change. Volunteers (organised by BTCV) also work in Richmond on separate projects: the close relationship between the two arms of BTCV helps ensure that there is no friction between the professional and voluntary workers.

Extensive consultation was undertaken, before and after the contract was awarded, with evening meetings, publication of plans, and guided walks. Once BTCV had won the contract, their manager was also introduced to people at public meetings. The contract itself was written with a view to making it comprehensible to the general public. This open approach has been sustained, and public relations functions are written into the contract. As a result BTCV Enterprises have taken on various important commitments, including a woodland open day, and the availability of information leaflets. Their staff and sub-contractors are expected to wear identifiable clothing and to take time to speak with the public, answer questions and provide information within the course of their work.

In Richmond there has certainly been a change in public perception, at least as far as the nature sites are concerned. Because consultation was extensive, and CCT provided the first opportunity to undertake this work, public awareness has changed significantly, with people not only noticing the difference, but understanding the changes. For example, tree thinning has been much less controversial, with most people understanding the reasons for it.

Contact: Eve Risbridger,

The Ecology Office, London Borough of Richmond Upon Thames,

Langholm Lodge, 146 Petersham Road,

Richmond TW10 6UX

Tel: 0181 332 2184

3.34 Parks ranger service:

London Borough of Southwark

Key theme

◆ New skills

In 1994, the London Borough of Southwark introduced a new Parks Ranger Service to run parallel to the established Parks Warden Service, a continued service negotiated between the union and the council after CCT had been introduced. Under CCT, grounds maintenance was contracted out, leaving Parks Warden Service workers to carry out a few tasks which matched their horticultural skills. By and large, however, their positions, although secure, were in a real sense, redundant. Many were offered early retirement, some were redeployed but others hung on. As natural wastage from the Parks Warden Service occurred, new staff with environmental backgrounds were employed in the Parks Ranger Service to undertake and develop specific programmes to enhance public use of the parks. A principal parks ranger was appointed to oversee and develop this new orientation to parks in Southwark.

The Parks Ranger Service is based on models developed in national parks in the USA, and more recently in British national and country parks. However, in Southwark this model is taking on its own characteristics based on local needs and identities in an urban environment.

The key characteristics of the Parks Ranger Service are:

◆ A strong concept of management principles and team structures with clear job descriptions based on qualifications, competencies and skills with training components, performance measures and regular reviews;

◆ A commitment to developing NVQ standards for this new service which has the potential to become a model for other local authorities. These standards are being developed using a combination of leisure, sports and recreation standards and COSQUEC which emphasises competencies, quality assurance and service centred delivery;

◆ A vision and a willingness to invest in non-traditional roles of rangers. A ranger position with an emphasis on community development qualifications and competencies will be part of the establishment in mid-1996. There are also plans for rangers with qualifications, competencies and skills in: health promotion; public relations and marketing; arts; fund-raising and sponsorship (which takes in public relations/marketing but also includes knowledge of EU funding and European languages); officers to exploit the resources of the River Thames, its foreshore and the adjacent docklands in conjunction with other authorities; community safety officers; information technology officers to link parks by computer; education officers who can negotiate service agreements with local schools; and, in conjunction with architects, rangers with skills in planning for environmentally sustainable parks rangers' headquarters in each major park to provide visibility and a commitment to a green building programme.

Many of these are still in the planning stages, but it presents a dynamic alternative to traditional views of what a modern urban parks service can offer.

Contact: Stephen Harrison,
Principal Parks Ranger,
London Borough of Southwark,
Chumleigh Gardens, Albany Road,
Burgess Park, Southwark, London SE5 0RJ
Tel: 0171 277 4068

3.35 Community involvement: St George's Gardens,

London Borough of Camden

Key theme

◆ Community involvement

St George's Gardens was the first burial ground in London not attached to a church. It is a delightful 'hidden jewel' of just over one acre, containing a number of impressive burial vaults, winding paths, ancient plane trees, much shrubbery, and grassed areas where in the summer lots of people sunbathe and picnic, coming from nearby colleges, office buildings and from the many local houses, flats, and apartment blocks. Even in winter it is a busy thoroughfare.

The site is managed by Camden Council, although it is still consecrated ground and owned by the church. It is subject to routine maintenance, now contracted out to a private company, as part of a borough-wide CCT arrangement. Dismayed by the continuing decline of the open space - vandalism to the vaults, collapsing tombs and walls, poor seating, overgrown shrubbery and lack of weed control - local residents have formed a friends group to propose an action plan of restoration and better maintenance. The money available to the contractor to maintain the space - basic grass cutting, emptying of bins, sweeping up leaves - seems inadequate to maintain it to a high quality, apparently the result of using a contract which the council are unable to monitor. It should be noted that the Friends of St George's Gardens claim that 'all these assaults on the physical artefacts have only really occurred since the gardens lost their resident gardener. Comparing the balance of his 'capitation cost' with the cost of repair and inanimate security would be interesting.'

The main issue is whether the unique site, with complicated past histories of ownership, important heritage elements, a complex ecology of flora and fauna, and patterns of use and abuse - for while it is very popular with hundreds if not thousands of local residents, students and workers, it is also used by prostitutes and drug-dealers - can be managed within a broad-brush CCT maintenance contract. The answer is probably not. This is precisely the kind of site that needs new forms of partnership management, with a dedicated programme of capital and revenue expenditure, which the local authority alone cannot afford; and CCT has not appeared to offer any improvement. The friends group do not wish to 'take over' the site, and are happy for the local authority to be ultimately responsible for its stewardship; but they do want to find a way of providing a local solution to a uniquely local asset.

Summary

◆ Formation of friends group committed to local distinctiveness of park

◆ Friends group has drawn up a Draft Management Plan for St George's Gardens

Contact: Jane Monahan,
Friends of St George's Gardens,
c/o 62 Marchmont Street,
London WC1N 1AB

3.36 Urban ranger and countryside warden service:

Stockport MBC

Key themes

◆ New skills

◆ Health

The Metropolitan Borough of Stockport has re-organised a section of its parks department into an Urban Ranger and Countryside Warden Service comprising approximately 40 full-time permanent staff with approximately 20 seasonal assistant rangers. The manager of this service is ultimately responsible to the Director of Leisure.

The provision of rangers and wardens is based on a team-based approach, with 20 urban rangers in four teams each under a

team leader. Each team is located in a park in one of four different quarters of the borough. In addition there are 10 countryside wardens.

In addition to monitoring and controlling, the job descriptions of the urban rangers emphasise close work with local playgroups and schools, bulb-planting programmes, environmental education, as well as organising an extensive programme of activities for the parks. The rangers also work in partnership with the Youth Service, and work with local drug action groups and provide drop-in centres for teenagers.

A recent development has been the commissioning of a series of leaflets and maps outlining guided walks for each locality, with 10 minute, 20 minute and longer walks recommended for those whose health would benefit from this encouragement. This programme is being undertaken jointly with local health providers, and the leaflets will be available for doctors to issue 'on prescription'.

Summary points

◆ New professional skills prioritising work with children and young people

◆ Joint work with health providers to encourage walking by developing local maps and guided walks available 'on prescription'

Contact: Bernard Sheridan, Manager,
Urban & Countryside Service,
Metropolitan Borough of Stockport,
Town Hall, Stockport SK1 3XE
Tel: 0161 474 4420

3.37 Developing a service plan:
Walsall Arboretum

Key theme
◆ Individual park management plan

Walsall Arboretum, the town's premier park, has been improved over the last four years. In 1995 it won a Government Charter Mark for the excellence and diversity of its services. It is one of the first public parks to win such an award.

Criteria for the Charter Mark
The application for the Charter Mark was made under the following criteria:

◆ Standards;

◆ Information and openness;

◆ Choice and consultation;

◆ Courtesy and helpfulness;

◆ Putting things right;

◆ Value for money;

◆ Customer satisfaction;

◆ Measurable improvements in the quality of service;

◆ Innovations.

The management approach is outlined in the Arboretum Service Plan. It includes:

◆ Public Surveys;

◆ Detailed appraisals of past service delivery;

◆ Health and Safety guidelines.

A Customer Service Contract is publicly available and is issued to all hirers of facilities of the Arboretum, including events organisers and sports clubs.

A re-investment programme
As a result of the parks review carried out in 1989 a decision was taken to re-invest in the Arboretum. One of the main attractions of the Arboretum is its illuminations which attract 300,000 visitors each year. The re-investment in the park included a massive refurbishment of the children's playground. The department secured significant grants from the European Regional Development Fund in order to re-develop the playground. The playground which is extensive and includes a lido is supervised during the summer months and the authority also provides play activities and temporary play workers.

The Arboretum, which in many ways draws inspiration from the older pleasure gardens, is the venue for many events and activities. Some are run by community groups, others, such as the Illuminations and music events are staged by Walsall Leisure and Community Services' in-house events team.

The illuminations

The Walsall illuminations were introduced into the Arboretum in 1951 as part of the Festival of Britain celebrations and they have been run as an annual attraction since then. The illuminations are on for a 6 week period in the autumn, with a programme of live entertainment. The events are charged for and in 1995 the average full-price ticket for evening events was £2.50.

For the past 6 years visitor surveys have been carried out. The research provides a long-term picture of the illuminations and can pick up underlying trends. It can also test the popularity of new features, such as the laser light show, mentioned by half the people interviewed in the most recent survey, as the highlight of the year's show.

Park management

Overall, the park attracts one million visitors a year. An area park manager, supported by four community park wardens manage the park and co-ordinate the work of other agencies in the park.

The Community Park Wardens have received customer care training as part of the Department's training policy. They have also undertaken a "Welcome Host" training course developed nationally by the English Tourist Board and implemented locally through the Regional Heart of England Tourist Board.

Community park wardens wear a distinctive uniform, with name badges and all carry mobile phones. Photographs of the staff on duty are displayed on a 'Welcome Board' at the entrance to the park. Weekly team briefings take place to ensure that all staff are kept fully informed about changes in the park and in the department as a whole. This also allows staff to report back users views and comments made during the week. It ensures that the staff are fully briefed to answer questions from park-users.

The process of applying for the Charter Mark was a useful way of concentrating staff thinking on the use and potential of Walsall's main town centre park. A service plan has been produced for the Arboretum to provide a clear framework and to enable closer working relationships with other agencies responsible for the operation of facilities within the park. The improvements in the park are categorised into four main areas:

◆ Fabric of the park;

◆ Environmental issues;

◆ Services to customers;

◆ The Arboretum as a venue for events.

Future plans

Future plans for the park include developing it as a 'healthier life style' park. There are plans to expand on the "healthy eating" initiative introduced by the Catering DSO and to promote the park as a place to visit for exercise. The park will also be the site for an initiative for recycling waste, thus embracing sustainable development issues.

Staff plan to introduce a 'walksafe' scheme. A successful scheme already operates in the borough's countryside sites which enables like minded people to team up and enjoy a walk.

Private sector partnership to develop and improve facilities over the next few years is also planned.

Summary points

◆ The process of applying for a Charter Mark is a useful way of concentrating thinking about how to improve the park;

◆ The market research provides valuable information that can be used to inform future development programmes. It reveals long-term trends and indicates a need to vary the programming and to promote the event each year;

◆ The service plan provides a clear framework for staff and for agencies and operators within the park.

Contact: David Brown,
Area Supervisor, Walsall Arboretum,
Walsall MBC, Leisure & Community Services,
Civic Centre, Darwall Street,
Walsall WS1 1TZ
Tel: 01922 724226

3.38 Urban wildlife groups in parks:

The Urban Wildlife Partnership

Key themes

◆ Community involvement

◆ Partnership funding

◆ Environmental education

Voluntary organisations such as Urban Wildlife Groups have, over recent years, become more involved in the management of wildlife areas within urban parks. The Urban Wildlife Partnership is a co-ordinating body, providing information and advice to its 92 Urban Wildlife Groups (amongst other member organisations). The Urban Wildlife Partnership has noted the trend amongst Urban Wildlife Groups to become involved in urban parks and is setting up a Parks Programme to further the work of Urban Wildlife Groups specifically in urban parks, and to establish good practice in the partnership arrangements between groups, residents and local authorities. The Urban Wildlife Partnership wish to explore and to promote Urban Wildlife Groups as a means of extending community involvement in parks and other urban open spaces.

Although all the groups take some aspect of wildlife as their focus, many now recognise that wildlife concerns are but one aspect of a successful park which can be balanced with other activities. Groups such as the Parks Regeneration Partnership in Sheffield have, in partnership with the City Council and other voluntary organisations in the city, made a commitment to improving the parks as a whole, recognising that the wildlife features of urban parks will work better in a park that is well used and well managed, rather than one that is displaying signs of decline. The majority of wildlife projects include an element of environmental education. In most cases the sites created are used by schools and other groups for educational projects.

The Wildlife Groups often gain the support and involvement of other local wildlife or conservation organisations and local residents. They can also apply for grant aid from schemes such as those run by the Civic Trust, English Nature, Shell Better Britain and so on. Several wildlife projects have, in partnership with local authorities, been able to fund a wardening post.

Projects such as the Oxford Urban Wildlife Group have, in partnership with Oxford City Council and other local groups, produced a five year park management plan to use derelict allotments to create a new nature park. The city leased the site to the Wildlife Group for a 'peppercorn' rent and have provided advice, assistance, trees and other equipment. The Boundary Brook Nature Park now includes a demonstration wildlife garden and organic allotments. It has won many local awards and received good local press coverage. The Wildlife Group have raised money from a variety of grants and are able to pay for a warden in the park.

The Bolton Wildlife Project has worked in close partnership with Bolton Metro Leisure Services to create several nature areas. Thomas Park is within the Bolton City Challenge area, and is the site for the local registry office. The volunteers and children working for Bolton Wildlife Project have designed and created a wildflower meadow and planted native bulbs and shrubs in the park. The project plans to link with Bolton City Challenge and hopes to be able to offer NVQ training in Landscape Ecology to trainees. Wildlife areas will be created as part of a management plan for the whole park, integrating more formal parts of the park, used particularly for wedding photographs, with wildlife areas.

There are dozens of examples of small scale partnerships between local authorities and local conservation groups carrying out innovative projects which help create community involvement in parks. However, there are occasional conflicts between wildlife groups and maintenance contractors. For example, contract specifications which do not allow for flexibility in mowing regimes can result in damage to wildlife areas, and even those contractors who are sympathetic can be restricted by reasons of cost to becoming too involved in the work of wildlife groups.

Many voluntary wildlife groups are tied to larger networks such as the Urban Wildlife Partnership or the Environment City Programme, who are pioneering work on environmental issues in urban areas, such as the development of 'sustainability indicators'. These networks are likely to become increasingly important in the development of ideas related to Agenda 21, and the ways in which parks can become a focus for questions of urban sustainability, environmental education and new forms of voluntary organisation.

Contact: Chris Gordon,
The Urban Wildlife Partnership, Witham Park Industrial Estate, Waterside South,
Lincoln LN5 7JR
Tel: 01522 544400

Appendix 1

Bibliography

ADLO, (1990) Ground Maintenance and Competitive Tendering Report, Association of Direct Labour Organisations, Manchester

ADLO, (1993) A Tale of Two Cities: A Study of Client/Contractor relationships for Grounds Maintenance, Association of Direct Labour Organisations, Manchester

ADLO, (1991) Sports and Leisure Management, Ensuring Contractor Performance, Association of Direct Labour Organisations, Manchester

Audit Commission, (1988) Competitive Management of Parks and Green Spaces, HMSO

Baines, Chris, (1986) The Wild Side of Town, BBC

Bell, Sandra (1995) Watch this Space, London Boroughs Association

Burgess, Jacquelin and Harrison, Carolyn(1987) Nature in the city - popular values for a living world, Journal of Environment Management, Vol. 25

Burgess, Jacquelin, Harrison Carolyn, and Limb, Melanie(1988) People, Parks and the Urban Green: a study of popular meanings and values for open spaces in the City, in Urban Studies (25), pp 455-473.

Burton Nick (1993) Urban Parks Wardening, ILAM

Centre for Study of Environmental Change (1994) Leisure Landscapes, CPRE

Cirell, Stephen & Bennett, John, (1995) The Problem of Cartels and restrictive Trade Practices in the Performance of Public Services, unpublished paper, Eversheds, Leeds

Comedia & Demos (1995) Park Life: Urban Parks & Social Renewal

Countryside Commission (1994) Securing a Greener Future for London

CPRE (1993) Sense & Sustainability

Commission of the European Communities, (1990) Green Paper on the Urban Environment.

CSEC (1993) Public Perceptions and the Nuclear Waste Industry in West Cumbria, report to Cumbria County Council, CSEC, Lancaster University

CSEC (1995) Public Perceptions of Sustainability in Lancashire, report to Lancashire County Council, CSEC, Lancaster University

CSEC (1994) Leisure Landscapes. Leisure, Culture and the English Countryside: Challenges and Conflicts, report for the Council for the Protection of Rural England, CSEC, Lancaster University

DoE, HMSO (1988) Creating Development Trusts

DoE (1994) Quality in Town and Country

DoE (1995) Involving Communities in Urban and Rural Regeneration, Pieda plc

Dunk, Julie & Rugg, Julie (1994) The Management of Old Cemetery Land, Shaw & Sons

DoE, HMSO (1987) Greening City Sites, Good Practice in Urban Regeneration

DoE, HMSO (1988) Improving Urban Areas, Good Practice in Urban Regeneration

Flint, Rosamund (1985) Encouraging Wildlife in Urban Parks, The London Wildlife Trust. Printed by Gordon Press

GLC (1986) Open Space in London, Habitat Handbook No2

Glasgow City Council, (1996) A New Vision, A New Future: Parks and Open Spaces Strategy.

GMB Trade Union (1993) Grounds for Concern

Johnston, Jacklyn (1990) Nature Areas for City People , Ecology Handbook 14, London Ecology Unit

Jacobs, M (1995) Sustainability and Socialism, London, SERA

Lancashire County Council (1995) Public Perceptions and Sustainability in Lancashire. Centre for Study of Environmental Change, Lancaster University

Llewelyn-Davies (1992) Open Space Planning in London , Planning & Environmental Trust Associates Ltd, LPAC

Local Government Management Board (1993), A Framework for Local Sustainability, London, LGMB

Local Government Management Board (1995), CCT Information Service Report (Ground Maintenance section), December 1995, London, LGMB

Marjone, G (1989) Evidence, Argument and Persuasion in the Policy Process, London, Basic Books

LGIU (1994) CCT On The Record, Local Government Information Unit, London

The National Trust (1995) Linking People and Place

Nicholson-Lord, David (1987) The Greening of the Cities, RKP

Power, M (1994) The Audit Explosion, London, Demos

The Royal Parks Agency (1995) People Using the Royal Parks, prepared by the Centre for Leisure and Tourism Studies, University of North London

Sibley, Peter (1995) Contemporary Problems of Historic Public Parks, Dissertation for Architectural Association Diploma, unpublished

SOLACE (1995) The Renaissance of Local Government, Society of Local Authority Chief Executives, London

Stewart, J (1995) Innovation in Democratic Practice in Local Government, Birmingham, INLOGOV

Swan, Bill (1994) The Effects of Compulsory Competitive Tendering of Grounds Maintenance on Urban Park Quality, MSc thesis, University of Reading, unpublished

Swan, Bill (1995) 'For Better or For Worse' Horticulture Week, January 19, 1995.

Titman Wendy (1994) Special Places, Special People. Learning through Landscapes

Turner, Tom (1991) Towards a Green Strategy For London, LPAC The

Victorian Society / Garden History Society (1993) Public Prospects

Walsh, K and Davies, H, Competition and Service: The Impact of the Local Government Act 1988, London, HMSO

Ward, Colin (1990) The Child in the City,   Bedford Square Press

Welch, David (1991) Management of Urban Parks, Longman

Appendix 2

Sources of information

Association of Direct Labour Organisations
4th Floor, Olympic House, Whitworth Street, Manchester M1 5WG
Tel: 0161 236 8433

Association of District Councils
26 Chapter Street, London SW1P 4ND
Tel: 0171 233 6868

Association of Metropolitan Authorities
35 Great Smith Street, London SW1P 3BJ
Tel: 0171 222 8100

Association for Environment Conscious Building
Windlake House, The Pump Field, Coaley, Glos GL11 5DX
Tel: 01453 890757

Black Environment Network
Regent's Wharf, 8 All Saint's Road, London N1 9RL
Tel: 0171 713 6161

British Trust for Conservation Volunteers
36 St Mary's Street, Wallingford, Oxfordshire OX10 0EU
Tel: 01491 839766

Camlin Lonsdale
15 Peel Street, Marsden, Huddersfield HD7 6B
Tel: 01484 841000

Centre for Accessible Environments Nutmeg House,
60 Gainsford Street, London SE1 2NY
Tel: 0171 357 8182

Centre for the Study of Environmental Change
Lancaster University, Lonsdale College, Lancaster LA1 4YN
Tel: 01524 592658

Civic Trust
17 Carlton House Terrace, London SW1Y 5AW
Tel: 0171 930 0914

Comedia
The Round, Bournes Green, Nr Stroud, Gloucestershire GL6 7NL
Tel: 01452 770624

Common Ground
44 Earlham Street, London WC2H 9LA
Tel: 0171 379 3109

Community Development Foundation
60 Highbury Grove, London N5 2AG
Tel: 0171 226 5375

Community Land & Workspaces Services Ltd
61/71 Collier Street, London N1 9BE
Tel: 0171 833 2909

Community Service Volunteers Environment
17 Midland Road, Bristol Bs2 0JT
Tel: 0117 955 9409

COSQUEC
The Red House, Pillows Green, Staunton, Gloucestershire GL19 3NU
Tel: 01452 840825

Department of the Environment
2 Marsham Street, London SW1P 3EB
Tel: 0171 276 3000

English Heritage
23 Savile Row, London W1X 1AB
Tel: 0171 973 3000

English Nature
Northminster House, Peterborough PE1 1UA
Tel: 01733 340345

The Environment Council
21 Elizabeth Street, London SW1W 9RP
Tel: 0171 824 8411

Friends of the Earth
26-28 Underwood Street, London N1 7JQ
Tel: 0171 490 1555

Garden History Society
5 The Knoll, Hereford HR1 1RU
Tel: 01432 354479

Groundwork Foundation
85/87 Cornwall Street, Birmingham B3 3BY
Tel: 0121 236 8565

Henry Doubleday Research Association
Ryton Organic Gardens, Ryton-on-Dunsmore, Coventry CV8 3LG
Tel: 01203 303517

Horticultural Therapy
Goulds Ground, Vallis Way, Frome, Somerset BA11 3DW
Tel: 01373 464782

Institute of Advanced Architectural Studies,
Landscape and Gardens University of York, The King's Manor, York YO1 2EP
Tel: 01904 433949

Institute of Leisure & Amenity Management
ILAM House, Lower Basildon, Reading, Berkshire RG8 9NE
Tel: 01491 874222

Landscape Design Trust
13a West Street, Reigate, Surrey RH2 9BL
Tel: 01737 225374

The Landscape Institute
6/7 Barnard Mews, London SW11 1QU
Tel: 0171 738 9166

Learning Through Landscapes
Southside Offices, The Law Courts, Winchester, Hampshire SO23 9DL
Tel: 01962 846258

National Federation of City Farms
The Greenhouse, Hereford Street, Bedminster, Bristol BS3 4NA
Tel: 0117 923 1800

National Heritage Memorial Fund
10 St James's Street, London SW1A 1EF
Tel: 0171 930 0963

National Playing Fields Association
25 Ovington Square, London SW3 1LQ
Tel: 0171 584 6445

National Urban Forestry Unit
Red House, Hill Lane, Great Barr, Sandwell, West Midlands B43 6LZ
Tel: 0121 358 1414

Open Spaces Society
25a Bell Street, Henley-on-Thames, Oxfordshire RG9 2BA
Tel: 01491 573535

Trust for Urban Ecology
167 Rotherhithe Street, London SE16 1EJ
Tel: 0171 237 9165

The Wildlife Trusts
The Green, Witham Park, Waterside South, Lincoln LN5 7JR
Tel: 01522 544400

The Women's Environmental Network
22 Highbury Grove, London N5 2EA
Tel: 0171 354 8823

Printed in the United Kingdom for HMSO.
Dd.0302181, 3/961, C13, 3400, 5673, 347231.